Swift Quick
Syntax Reference

Matthew Campbell

Apress®

Swift Quick Syntax Reference

ISBN-13 (pbk): 978-1-4842-0440-5

ISBN-13 (electronic): 978-1-4842-0439-9

Trademarked names, logos, and images may appear in this book. Rather than use a trademark symbol with every occurrence of a trademarked name, logo, or image we use the names, logos, and images only in an editorial fashion and to the benefit of the trademark owner, with no intention of infringement of the trademark.

The use in this publication of trade names, trademarks, service marks, and similar terms, even if they are not identified as such, is not to be taken as an expression of opinion as to whether or not they are subject to proprietary rights.

While the advice and information in this book are believed to be true and accurate at the date of publication, neither the authors nor the editors nor the publisher can accept any legal responsibility for any errors or omissions that may be made. The publisher makes no warranty, express or implied, with respect to the material contained herein.

Publisher: Heinz Weinheimer
Lead Editor: Michelle Lowman
Development Editor: Douglas Pundick
Technical Reviewer: Charles Cruz
Editorial Board: Steve Anglin, Ewan Buckingham, Gary Cornell, Louise Corrigan, James T. DeWolf, Jonathan Gennick, Jonathan Hassell, Robert Hutchinson, Michelle Lowman, James Markham, Matthew Moodie, Jeff Olson, Jeffrey Pepper, Douglas Pundick, Ben Renow-Clarke, Dominic Shakeshaft, Gwenan Spearing, Matt Wade, Steve Weiss
Coordinating Editor: Melissa Maldonado
Copy Editor: Kim Wimpsett
Compositor: SPi Global
Indexer: SPi Global
Artist: SPi Global
Cover Designer: Anna Ishchenko

Distributed to the book trade worldwide by Springer Science+Business Media New York, 233 Spring Street, 6th Floor, New York, NY 10013. Phone 1-800-SPRINGER, fax (201) 348-4505, e-mail orders-ny@springer-sbm.com, or visit www.springeronline.com. Apress Media, LLC is a California LLC and the sole member (owner) is Springer Science + Business Media Finance Inc (SSBM Finance Inc). SSBM Finance Inc is a Delaware corporation.

For information on translations, please e-mail rights@apress.com, or visit www.apress.com.

Apress and friends of ED books may be purchased in bulk for academic, corporate, or promotional use. eBook versions and licenses are also available for most titles. For more information, reference our Special Bulk Sales–eBook Licensing web page at www.apress.com/bulk-sales.

Any source code or other supplementary material referenced by the author in this text is available to readers at www.apress.com. For detailed information about how to locate your book's source code, go to www.apress.com/source-code/.

To my girls, Stacie and Keira.

Contents at a Glance

Contents

About the Author

Matthew Campbell is a data analyst, programmer, and published technology author with 14 years of experience in research data analysis, mobile applications, Windows applications, and web services.

He spent six years as an indy application developer with a grand total of twelve applications, including two featured apps on the Apple App Store.

Matt holds a master's degree in information systems and a bachelor's degree in psychology. He is a lifelong learner who is excited about learning new domain knowledge, processes, and technologies.

About the Technical Reviewer

Charles Cruz is a mobile application developer for the iOS, Windows Phone, and Android platforms. He graduated from Stanford University with bachelor's and master's degrees in engineering. He lives in Southern California and runs a photography business with his wife (www.bellalentestudios.com). When not doing technical things, he plays lead guitar in an original metal band (www.taintedsociety.com). Charles can be reached at codingandpicking@gmail.com and @CodingNPicking on Twitter.

Introduction

The expressions of the WWDC 2014 audience quickly changed from excitement and enthusiasm to looks of shock, horror, and awe. At this WWDC, after a succession of ever-surprising announcements, Apple ended the conference by announcing a completely new programming language designed entirely for Mac and iOS applications. This programming language is named Swift, which is what I have written about in this book.

The audience members' looks of shock and horror were understandable in context. Most of the developers at that conference had spent the past six years mastering the previous, relatively obscure programming language used to develop apps called Objective-C. The people sitting in those seats were world-class experts in a programming language that was just declared dead right in front of them.

What many of these developers probably had long since forgotten was just how difficult it is for most people to use Objective-C at first. Objective-C is also missing many features that other programmers take for granted such as tuples and generics. This is likely why that over the summer of 2014 many developers would become quite enthusiastic about adopting Swift in their projects.

It didn't take long for me to get on board with Swift. My initial reaction was relief that Apple decided to clean up the syntax, remove the clutter associated with Objective-C, and eject nonmainstream notions like messaging objects. I could tell immediately that the students I teach would take to Swift way more quickly than Objective-C.

This is one of the reasons I was so excited to write this book with Apress. Swift is absolutely the programming language that will take iOS and Mac into the future. Swift is a dramatic improvement to the application ecosystem. If you were turned off from making applications before because of Objective-C, now is the time to give making your app another go.

This book is written for programmers who want to get up to speed quickly in Swift. I made an effort to keep chapter headings specific, simple, and clear so you can go right to the area that you need to focus on. Chapters are short and focus on the syntax, but concepts are briefly illustrated at times when the information is crucial to the programming concepts that I'm presenting.

Since Swift is so new, I didn't make many assumptions about your technical background, so anyone with a general understanding of programming will benefit from this book. If you know what loops, functions, and objects are, you can follow the content here. Any niche or advanced programming constructs will be explained so you can follow along.

Good luck with your app! I hope that this book will help you appreciate Swift and see how this new language will make your life and your app much better.

Chapter 1

Hello World

I will start our conversation about Swift with the venerable Hello World program. However, you need to get some things in place before I can do that. Most importantly, you need a Mac app that will help you write and test Swift code. This Mac app is called Xcode.

Xcode

Xcode is a free app that you can download from the Apple App Store. Xcode gives you all the tools that you need to build applications for the Mac and iOS devices. These tools include a code editor, debugging tools, and everything else you need to turn your Swift code into an app.

> **Note**   Xcode requires a Mac with OS X 10.9.3 or OS X 10.10. You cannot install Xcode on a Windows- or Linux-based computer.

Install Xcode

To install Xcode, go to the Mac App Store by selecting your Mac's menu bar, clicking the Apple symbol, and then clicking App Store. Use the App Store search feature to locate Xcode by typing the word *Xcode* into the text box next to the hourglass. Press Return to search for Xcode. You will be presented with a list of apps, and Xcode should be the first app in the list. Install Xcode by clicking the button with the word *free* next to the Xcode icon. The word *free* changes to *installed* once it's ready to go, as shown in Figure 1-1.

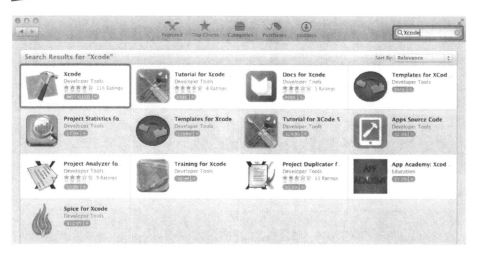

Figure 1-1. Downloading Xcode from the App Store

> **Note**   Xcode version 6 is required to do Swift programming. By the time
> this book is released, Xcode 6 should be available in the Apple App Store,
> and you should be able to get it by following the previous instructions.
> However, at the time of this writing, Xcode 6 is still in beta and available
> only to registered Apple developers who can download it from the Apple
> developer web site at `http://developer.apple.com`.

Create a New Playground

Playgrounds are a workspace that you use to quickly prototype Swift code.
The examples in this book will assume that you are using playgrounds to
follow along. You use Xcode to make a playground.

Open Xcode by going to your `Applications` folder and clicking the Xcode
app. You will be presented with a welcome screen. Click the text "Get
started with a playground" to build your playground (see Figure 1-2).

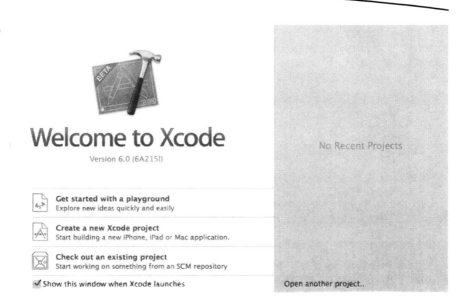

Figure 1-2. Xcode welcome screen

You will be presented with a Save As screen, as shown in Figure 1-3. Use this screen to choose a name and location for your Swift playground.

Figure 1-3. Playground Save As screen

Once you choose your playground's name and folder location, Xcode will present a code editor with some boilerplate code already filled in for you (see Figure 1-4).

Figure 1-4. Playground boilerplate

Your first playground has been created, and you already have a sort of Hello World program coded for you. Well, not exactly. Your code says "Hello, playground," as you can see in Listing 1-1.

Listing 1-1. Hello Playground

```
// Playground - noun: a place where people can play
import Cocoa
var str = "Hello, playground"
```

You use a playground by typing in code in the left area of the code editor. You can immediately see results appear on the right in the playground. To create a Hello World program, all you need to do is type in the phrase "Hello World" (including the quotes) into the playground code editor (see Listing 1-2).

Listing 1-2. Hello World

```
// Playground - noun: a place where people can play
import Cocoa
var str = "Hello, playground"
"Hello World"
```

When you type in "Hello World", you will immediately see the output "Hello World" appear on the right. See Figure 1-5 as a reference.

Figure 1-5. *"Hello World" output*

Chapter 2

Declaring Constants and Variables

While you can use values like the string "Hello World" from the previous chapter or a number like 3.14 directly in code, usually you assign values like these to either a variable or a constant. You can give values a convenient name using variables and constants in Swift.

Variables can change their values over time, while constants get an assigned value and keep that value throughout the execution of a program. Both variables and constants can store only one type of data.

Constants

Let's reproduce the Hello World example from Chapter 1 using a constant. Listing 2-1 shows how to store the string "Hello World" in a constant named s1.

Listing 2-1. Hello World Constant

```
let s1:String = "Hello World"
```

The first part of the constant declaration is the let keyword. The let keyword lets you know that you are working with a constant. The next part is the constant name s1. You will use the constant name s1 to refer to this constant in your code from now on.

You also have the type declaration :String. The type declaration tells you what data type the constant stores. Since you used the type declaration :String, you know that you can store strings (a sequence of characters) in the constant s1.

The next part is the assignment operator =, which assigns a value to the constant s1. The value here is a string enclosed in quotes, `"Hello World"`.

If you use a playground to prototype the code here, you will see that it immediately reports the value of the s1 constant on the right side of the screen.

You can reference a constant by using its name. To get the value of s1, you can just type in the constant name anywhere in your code. Try it right now by typing s1 into your playground (see Listing 2-2).

Listing 2-2. Referencing Constants

```
s1
```

You will be using constants more as you learn about the capabilities of Swift.

Constants Are Immutable

Let's say you would rather have "Hello World" print as "Hello World!" (with an exclamation point). Since s1 is a constant, you cannot simply change the value or this code would cause an error (see Listing 2-3).

Listing 2-3. Error Caused by Assigning a Value to a Constant

```
s1 = "Hello World!"
```

When you need to change a value when a program runs, you must use a variable.

Variables

Variables are mostly used like constants but with two key differences. The first is that variables use the var keyword instead of the let keyword when variables are being declared. The second difference is that variable values can change.

Listing 2-4 shows an example of a variable s2 that can change value over time.

Listing 2-4. Variable Declaration

```
var s2:String = "Hello World"
```

As you can see in Listing 2-4, you use the var keyword to specify variables. Variables also don't require that you immediately assign a value to them, so you could have waited to assign the "Hello World" string to s2.

Variables Are Mutable

Since s2 is a variable, you can change its value. So, if you wanted to say "Hello World" in Spanish instead, you could change the value of s2 as shown in Listing 2-5.

Listing 2-5. Changing Variable Value

```
s2 = "Hola Mundo"
```

Now if you type s2 into your playground, you will see the value "Hola Mundo" appear on the right.

Type Inference

In the previous examples, you clearly spelled out the data type for both the variables and the constants. However, Xcode can figure this out for you based on what value you assign to the variable or constant. This is called *type inference*. This means you could have omitted the :String from your declarations and instead use something like Listing 2-6.

Listing 2-6. Type Inference

```
var s3 = "Hallo Welt"
```

Data Types

Swift supports more than the String data type. You also work with numbers and booleans. Table 2-1 describes the common Swift data types.

Table 2-1. Swift Data Types

Data Type	Description
String	Sequence of characters
Int	Whole number
Float	Number with fractional component
Double	Bigger number with fractional component
Bool	True or false value

See Listing 2-7 for examples of how to use these data types.

Listing 2-7. Swift Data Types

```
let s:String = "Hey There"
let i:Int = -25
let f:Float = 3.14
let d:Double = 99.99
let b:Bool = true
```

Chapter 3

Printing Variables and Constants

When you are prototyping your code with playgrounds, you automatically get output for any variable or constant that you are working with. But, if you are coding an application, you will need to use special functions to print out values to the console screen.

Since playgrounds have no console window, you will need to create a new Mac command-line tool to print values to a console screen.

Creating a Command-Line Tool

Open Xcode 6 and then choose Create a new Xcode project from the welcome screen.

On the screen that appears, choose OS X ➤ Application ➤ Command Line Tool.

Click Next.

On the next screen, fill out the information required, including the name of the application. Be sure to choose Swift as the language. See Figure 3-1 for an example.

Choose options for your new project:

Product Name:	003-Printing-Variables-and-Constants
Organization Name:	MattjCamp
Organization Identifier:	com.mattjcamp
Bundle Identifier:	com.mattjcamp.-03-Printing-Variables-and...
Language:	Swift

Cancel   Previous   Next

Figure 3-1. Command tool information fields

Click Next.

Choose the folder location for your command tool application and then click Create.

The Command Line Tool Xcode project is a little bit more complicated than a playground. You are most interested in the Swift code file named main.swift. You should see this file in Xcode's folder view on the left part of your screen. Click the file main.swift. You should see a screen similar to Figure 3-2.

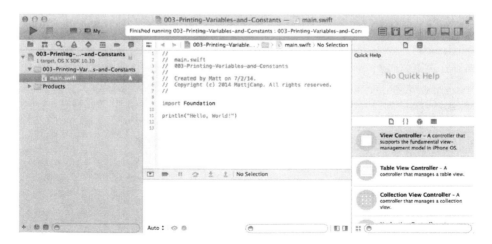

Figure 3-2. Command Tool Xcode project

In the middle of your screen you should see a code editor with a simple "Hello World!" line of code filled in.

Printing to the Console

The code that appears in `main.swift` contains the function that you will use to print out values to the console window: `println()`, as shown in Listing 3-1.

Listing 3-1. println()

```
import Foundation

println("Hello, World!")
```

To see the output of the `println()` function, click the big arrow in the upper-left area of your Xcode screen to build and run the command-line tool application. At the bottom of your screen, you should see the console window with the "Hello World!" message printed out.

> **Note**   If you adjusted your Xcode screens and ended up hiding your console window, you may need to use the controls located in the upper-right area of Xcode and on the bottom-center screen to reveal your console window. Figure 3-3 shows where these controls are located.

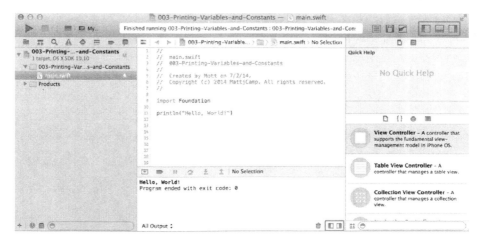

Figure 3-3. Showing/hiding Xcode windows

You can use `println()` to print strings like you have just seen, or you can print out variable and constant values, as shown in Listing 3-2.

Listing 3-2. Printing Variables

```
println(s)
```

While `println()` prints something out and then goes to the next line, `print()` will print out a value without moving to the next line in the console window, as shown in Listing 3-3.

Listing 3-3. print() Function

```
print("Print this")
print(" and ")
print("that")
```

The code in Listing 3-3 will print everything on one line like this:

```
Print this and that
```

String Interpolation

If you need to print out different variables, constants, literals, and expressions in a string on one line, you can use string interpolation. You do this by putting a forward slash (\) in front of a variable name in parentheses. For instance, let's say you have the constants from the end of Chapter 2 and want to print them out all in one line with a `println()` function, as shown in Listing 3-4.

Listing 3-4. String Interpolation

```
let i:Int = -25
let f:Float = 3.14
let d:Double = 99.99
let b:Bool = true

println("i = \(i), f = \(f), d = \(d), b = \(b)")
```

The code in Listing 3-4 will print out the following line:

```
i = -25, f = 3.14000010490417, d = 99.99, b = true
```

Chapter 4

Code Comments

You use code comments when you want to add information to your code. With Swift, you can add a one-line code comment, multiple-line code comments, and even nested code comments.

One-Line Code Comments

Use the double backslashes (//) to start a one-line code comment. See Listing 4-1 as an example.

Listing 4-1. One-Line Code Comment

```
//One line code comment
```

You can fill up one line with these types of comments.

Multiline Comments

One-line comments are fine for quick notes about code that may need some extra information provided. But when you want to add a lengthier description, you can write over many lines at once. To write a multiline comment, you start the comment with a backslash and asterisk (/*), write the comment, and end it with an asterisk and backslash (*/). See Listing 4-2.

Listing 4-2. Multiline Comments

```
/*
Multiple line code comment
Use this when you need to provide more detail
*/
```

Nested Code Comments

Swift supports nested comments. Nested comments allow you to quickly comment out large chunks of code that have code comments included in the code. You can use the same code comment symbols /* and */ with nested comments. For instance, let's assume you have two sets of two constants declared, each of which have their own comments. You could write that as shown in Listing 4-3.

Listing 4-3. Multiple Code Comments

```
/*
Define a and b constants
*/

let a = 1
let b = 2

/*
Define c and d constants
*/

let c = 3
let d = 4
```

You can comment out all of this code by enclosing everything in Listing 4-3 in code comments, as shown in Listing 4-4.

Listing 4-4. Nested Code Comments

```
/*
/*
Define a and b constants
*/

let a = 1
let b = 2

/*
Define c and d constants
*/

let c = 3
```

```
let d = 4

*/
```

None of the code in Listing 4-4 will execute, but if you remove the outermost comments, you can preserve the inner comments. This makes it easy to test code but keep any code comments you added previously.

Chapter 5

Numbers

Numbers have their own data types in Swift. Like with other programming languages, in Swift some number data types can store larger numbers than others, and numbers that have a fractional component are treated differently than numbers that are whole numbers.

Integers

Integers are whole numbers that may be either positive or negative. Integers don't have any decimal places. For example, 1, 2, and -9 are all integers. While there are several integer data types, you will usually use the Int data type. Int is used when you don't need to specify a size for the integer. Listing 5-1 shows two examples of declaring integers.

Listing 5-1. Declaring Integers

```
let i1:Int = 5
var i2 = 7
```

In Listing 5-1, i1 is an integer constant, while i2 is an integer variable.

Integer Sizes

Int will always conform to the largest native signed size. This means on 32-bit systems Int can store any integer from -2,147,483,648 to 2,147,483,648.

Unless you have a good reason, you should always use Int since this helps with interoperability (iOS has both 32-bit and 64-bit devices available).

If you do want to specify the integer size, you can use data types that correspond to the C data types such as Int8, Int16, Int32, Int64, UInt8, UInt16, UInt32, and UInt64.

In these data types, the numbers indicate the size of the integer. For example, Int8 means 8-bit, which gives you an integer range of -127 to 127. The data types that have a *U* as the first character are unsigned integers. These integers must be positive. UInt8 gives you a range of 0 to 255.

Floating-Point Numbers

Floating-point numbers can have decimal places. An example of a floating-point number is 9.99. To specify a floating-point number, you can use the Float data type, as shown in Listing 5-2.

Listing 5-2. Declaring Floating-Point Numbers

```
let f1:Float = 9.99
let f2 = 3.14
```

If you leave out the data type and include a number with decimal places, Swift will use type inference to assume you want a number with the Float data type.

Float is a 32-bit floating-point number, and you should use that when you don't require 64-bit precision. When you do require 64-bit precision, use the Double data type, as shown in Listing 5-3.

Listing 5-3. Declaring Double Floating-Point Numbers

```
let d1:Double = 1.2345
```

Chapter 6

Strings

A string is a sequence of characters, such as "Hello World!". Strings use the String data type, although you don't need to specify the data type to use a string, as shown in Listing 6-1.

Listing 6-1. Declaring Strings

```
var s1 = "Hello World!"
```

Unicode Characters

Strings can include any Unicode characters. To write single-byte Unicode characters, you must include \x before the two hexadecimal digits. Two-byte Unicode characters are prefixed with \u before four hexadecimal digits, and four-byte Unicode characters have \U written before eight hexadecimal digits.

Listing 6-2 shows an example of using Unicode characters.

Listing 6-2. Unicode Characters

```
let percentage = "\x{25}"
let snowflake = "\u{2744}"
let heart = "\u{0001F497}"
```

The code in Listing 6-1 will display a percentage sign, a snowflake, and a heart in your playground.

Character Data Type

Strings are collections of characters, and characters have their own data type called Character. Characters can have only one character, and you must explicitly declare your variable or constant as a Character. See Listing 6-3 for an example of how to declare a Character.

Listing 6-3. Character Declaration

```
let c1:Character = "A"
```

Concatenation

In Swift, you can combine strings and characters to create longer strings. Since a character can contain only one character, you can't combine strings or characters using a Character type variable.

If you think you want to have a string that you can add more characters to, make sure to declare the string as a String type variable with the var keyword. Constants cannot be modified.

Listing 6-4 shows an example of how you might start constructing an alphabet string based on characters and strings that you already have on hand.

Listing 6-4. String/Character Concatenation

```
//Declare characters and strings
let c1:Character = "A"
let c2:Character = "B"
let c3:Character = "C"
let c4:Character = "D"
let c5:Character = "E"
let s2 = "FGHIJ"

//Declare an empty string
var alphabet = String()

//Concatenate strings, characters and literals
alphabet = c1 + c2 + c3 + c4 + c5 + s2 + "KLMNOP"
```

If you're using a playground, you will see the first part of the alphabet appear on the right.

Also, if you look closely at the declaration for alphabet, you will see that this sets alphabet to String(). This is how you create an empty string in Swift. The last statement uses + signs to combine the strings, characters, and the string literal "LMNOP".

Comparing Strings

You can find out whether one string is equal to another with the equality comparison operator (==). If you do this, you will get a boolean (true or false) value back. If you wanted to see whether the alphabet variable contains the entire alphabet, you can use the comparison operator to test alphabet, as shown in Listing 6-5.

Listing 6-5. Comparing Strings

```
//returns boolean false
alphabet == "ABCDEFGHIJKLMNOPQRSTUVWXYZ"

//returns boolean true
alphabet == "ABCDEFGHIJKLMNOP"
```

> **Note**   Comparison operators are usually used with if statements, and both of these topics are covered later in the book (Chapters 15 and 25, respectively).

String Interpolation

As I discussed in Chapter 3, you can use string interpolation to insert values into strings to create new strings. These values can be numbers, other strings, and other types.

In addition to printing out interpolated strings to the console window with println(), you can create new strings with interpolation, as shown in Listing 6-6.

Listing 6-6. String Interpolation

```
let s3 = "Three Times Three = \(9) & the alphabet is \(alphabet)"
```

In Listing 6-6, you are creating a new string with string interpolation by inserting the value 9 and the value of the variable alphabet into the string "Three Times Three = & the alphabet is".

The value of s3 will be "Three Times Three = 9 & the alphabet is ABCDEFGHIJKLMNOP".

Chapter 7

Booleans

Boolean values can be either true or false. Booleans are used to help evaluate logical expressions. To declare a boolean value, you can assign a value immediately, or you can use the `Bool` data type to declare a boolean variable, as shown in Listing 7-1.

Listing 7-1. Declaring Booleans

```
var b1:Bool
let b2 = false
```

In Chapter 6, you saw how to make a comparison between two strings to get a boolean value. You can store the results of an equality comparison like that in a boolean variable or constant, as shown in Listing 7-2.

Listing 7-2. Storing Boolean Results

```
let alphabet = "ABCDEFGHIJKLMNOP"
let b4 = alphabet == "ABCDEFGHIJKLMNOP"
```

In Listing 7-2, the value of b4 is `true` because the two strings are the same; you can use this information later in the program by referencing b4. Listing 7-2 uses the equality operator that was introduced in the previous chapter, but you can do other types of tests and store the results in `Bool` variables. See Chapter 15 for a complete list of comparison operators you can use.

Booleans are particularly useful when used with `if` statements to control the flow of your program. You will learn more about `if` statements in Chapter 23.

Chapter 8

Tuples

Tuples are ordered lists of values. In Swift, you can group related elements together as a tuple, reducing the need to depend on complex types, objects, and immutable arrays.

Listing 8-1 shows how you would declare a tuple for a rectangle.

Listing 8-1. Declaring Tuples

```
let rectangle1 = (0, 0, 200, 100)
```

In Listing 8-1, you use the `let` keyword to declare a constant and give the constant the name `rectangle1`. After the assignment operator (=), you supply a comma-separated list of values enclosed in parentheses.

The value of `rectangle1` from Listing 8-1 would be (0, 0, 200, 100).

For greater clarity, you can annotate each value in the tuple list as shown in Listing 8-2.

Listing 8-2. Annotated Tuple

```
var rectangle2 = (x:0, y:0, width:200, height:100)
```

To pull an individual value out of a tuple, you can decompose the values and assign them to a constant, as shown in Listing 8-3.

Listing 8-3. Decomposed Tuple

```
let (a, b, c, d) = rectangle1

//prints 200
c
```

To decompose your tuple values, you can use the let keyword followed by a comma-separated list of variable names. Each name will be filled with the corresponding value from the tuple. You can now use these variables as usual. For instance, when you type c, the variable name from Listing 8-1, the value 200 from the tuple will appear.

To ignore some values in a tuple, you can replace a variable name with an underscore (_). So, if you needed only the x origin for the rectangle, you could do this as shown in Listing 8-4.

Listing 8-4. Ignoring Tuple Parts

```
var (e, _, _, _) = rectangle2

//prints 0
e
```

You can assign tuple values to either constants or variables, as you can see in Listing 8-4.

Chapter 9

Optionals

In situations where you can't be sure a variable has a value present, you can use optionals. An *optional* is a variable that can have either an assigned value or no value at all. Using optionals is an alternative to setting objects to `nil`. Optionals can be used with any type in Swift including numbers, strings, and objects.

You declare optionals like variables or constants, but you must include a ? after the type declaration (see Listing 9-1). Like variables and constants, the data type of an optional may be inferred.

Listing 9-1. String Optional Declaration

```
var s:String?
```

The variable s in Listing 9-1 is declared as an optional, and the starting value is `nil`.

Forced Unwrapping

If you are sure that an optional has a value, then you can use an exclamation point (!) to unwrap the value. For instance, if you know that s has a value, then you could unwrap s and use the value as shown in Listing 9-2.

Listing 9-2. Unwrapping

```
var s:String?

s = "ABC"

s!
```

You will see the value of s display on the right pane of your playground.

If you attempt to unwrap an optional that has no value, then you will get a runtime error, and your playground will stop functioning. Make sure the Assistant Editor is visible so you can see runtime errors (click Xcode ➤ View ➤ Show Assistant Editor). For this reason, you will want to test your optional with an if statement before attempting to unwrap the optional (Listing 9-3). See Chapter 23 for more information on if statements.

Listing 9-3. Testing Before Unwrapping Optionals

```
if s{
    "The value of s is "
    s!
}
else{
    "No value in s"
}
```

Optional Bindings

Optional bindings give you a way to test an optional and unwrap the optional in an if statement. Optional bindings will save you from explicitly unwrapping the optional inside your if statement. To rewrite Listing 9-3 with optional bindings, use the code in Listing 9-4.

Listing 9-4. Optional Bindings

```
if let myString = s{
    "The value of s is "
    myString
}else{
    "No value in s"
}
```

You can see in Listing 9-4 that you have a constant declaration right after the if statement so that you are both testing for nil and assigning a temporary constant that you can use in the code block if a value is present.

Chapter **10**

Type Aliases

You can add an alternative name for existing types using type aliases. This is something you might do if you want to make your API more expressive and clearer to other programmers. For instance, let's say you had a type of string that you wanted to treat as a note in your code. You could use a type alias to define Note as an alternative to String.

Use the typealias keyword to define a type alias, as shown Listing 10-1.

Listing 10-1. Type Alias

```
typealias Note = String
```

Now that you've defined the type alias, you can use the type Note in place of String when you are declaring new variables, constants, or optionals (see Listing 10-2).

Listing 10-2. Using Type Aliases

```
typealias Note = String

var n1:Note = "Today is the first day of our new project"
```

You can treat n1 as a string, which means you will have the same functionality as a string object. The only difference is that you can refer to certain strings as Note types, making the purpose of the notes clearer.

Some types like Int have functions associated with them. For instance, if you wanted to find out the maximum integer value that can be stored by an Int type, you could use the max function (Listing 10-3).

Listing 10-3. Int Max Function

```
Int.max
```

If you do this on your Mac, you will see a large number appear in the playground. If you set an alias for `Int`, any function available to `Int` will be available to the alias.

For instance, if you defined an alias for `Int` to represent speed, then you could do something like Listing 10-4.

Listing 10-4. Speed Max Function

```
typealias Speed = Int

Speed.max
```

Since you can treat `Speed` the same as `Int`, you can use the `max` function on `Speed`.

Chapter 11

Global and Local Variables

Most of the variables that you have been working with in the examples have had global scope. *Global scope* means that once the variable is declared, you can access its value from anywhere in your Swift program. This is in contrast to Objective-C, which couldn't have variables with global scope.

Scope Defined

Scope refers to a portion of a program. In other words, you can access variables only from the portion of the program where the variable has been declared. Portions of the program are defined by various Swift constructs such as if statements (Chapter 23), functions (Chapter 27), and classes (Chapter 30).

> **Note**   Scope applies broadly to other types in Swift as well as variables.

You will see curly brackets ({}) used with Swift constructs to define a scope for part of your program. Since you saw the if statement already in Chapter 9, Listing 11-1 uses that as an example to demonstrate scope.

Listing 11-1. If Statement Scope

```
let isTrue = true

if(isTrue){
    var myString = "This is a true statement"
    println(myString)
}
```

Listing 11-1 declares a boolean constant called `isTrue` and uses an `if` statement to test to see whether `isTrue` is set to a `true` value. If this statement is true, you define an area of scope with curly brackets ({}) and put the code that you want to execute in between the curly brackets.

If you look at the area in the curly brackets (the *scoped* area), you will see the variable that is declared is named `myString`. `myString` is a variable that is local to the scoped area.

This means you can access `myString` only in that scoped area. So, Listing 11-2 would cause an error.

Listing 11-2. Variable Out of Scope

```
let isTrue = true

if(isTrue){
    var myString = "This is a true statement"
    println(myString)
}

println(myString)
```

However, since `isTrue` is a global variable, you can use that anywhere in your program, including the scoped area after your `if` statement.

Variables remain in scope even when a scoped area itself has scoped portions. So, if you have an `if` statement that contains other `if` statements, then variables declared in the topmost scoped area are still accessible in the nested scoped areas.

Global Variables

The concept of scope is not unique to Swift, but I am discussing it here mainly because this is a feature that works differently than in Objective-C. In Swift, any variable or type that you declare in an area that is not scoped will be a global variable or type.

Chapter 12

Assertions

Assertions are a tool that you can use to help with your debugging efforts. Assertions work by testing a condition to see whether the condition is satisfied. If the condition is not satisfied, then a runtime error occurs, and the program stops executing. Assertions may have an optional message that is printed in the console window when the condition is not met.

To create an assertion, write the assertion shown in Listing 12-1.

Listing 12-1. Assert

```
var triangleSides = 4

assert(triangleSides == 3, "A triangle must have three sides")
```

The assert statement in Listing 12-1 is testing to make sure that the triangleSides variable has the correct number of sides. If triangleSides has three sides, nothing happens. If triangleSides has any other number of sides, the program stops running, and the text in the second part of the function appears in the console window.

> **Note**   It is hard to see how assertions work when you are working with a playground since your program doesn't really stop like it would if you were coding an app. However, you can see the console window in the playground by going to the Xcode menu bar and then clicking View ➤ Assistant Editor ➤ Show Assistant Editor. You will see the runtime error printed in the console window on the right.

Assertions are tested only in Debug mode since they are meant to help you when debugging your application. You use assertions when logical conditions that are possible would cause a fatal error in your application.

You can use any comparison operator (Chapter 15) or logical operator (Chapter 18) in your assertions.

Chapter **13**

Assignment Operators

When you want to initialize or update a value, you use the *assignment* operator (=). You saw this already when you learned to declare constants and variables with a value using the assignment operator (see Listing 13-1).

Listing 13-1. Declaring and Assigning Values

```
//Assigning a variable value
```

```
nstant value
```

the variable values at any time after the variable has been
he assignment operator (see Listing 13-2).

ng Values

```
a = 3
```

Of course, you cannot do this with a constant.

You can assign multiple values to multiple variables or constants on the same line to save space (see Listing 13-3).

Listing 13-3. Multiple Assignments

```
let (c, d) = (4, 5)
```

In Listing 13-3, c will equal 4, and d will equal 5.

To assign tuple values, you must supply the variable or constant with a comma-separated list of values enclosed in parentheses (see Listing 13-4).

Listing 13-4. Assigning Tuple Values

```
let e = (6, 7, 8)
```

The output that will appear in the right pane of your playground will be (.0 6, .1 7, .2 8).

When you need to extract a tuple value from a variable or constant, you can use an assignment operator to assign one of the tuple values to a new variable or constant. Every tuple value except the one you are interested in must be replaced with an underscore (_) character (see Listing 13-5).

Listing 13-5. Extract a Tuple Value

```
let (_,_,f) = e
```

Listing 13-5 will give you a new constant f that has the same value as the third value in the tuple e.

Compound Operators

The assignment operator is often combined with an arithmetic operator (see Chapter 14) when you want to perform an arithmetic operator and assign the result to the value in the same line of code (see Listing 13-6).

Listing 13-6. Compound Assignment/Arithmetic Operations

```
//Declare and assign i integer equal to 0
var i = 0

//Add 4 to i and assign result back to i
i+=4

//Multiple i by 2 and assign result back to i
i*=2
```

In Listing 13-6, you start off with an integer i that has a value of 0 and then use compound assignment/arithmetic operations to first add 4 to i and then multiply i by 2. You can use any arithmetic operation like this with the assignment operator.

Chapter 14

Arithmetic Operators

You use the *arithmetic* operators to do addition (+), subtraction (-), multiplication (*), and division (/). Generally, you use these operators in the same way you would in math (see Listing 14-1).

Listing 14-1. Arithmetic Operators

```
let r1 = 1 + 2
let r2 = 3 - 1
let r3 = 6 * 5
let r4 = 12 / 3
```

If you are using arithmetic operators on two integers, then you can expect an integer result by default. All of the examples in Listing 14-1 will result in integer output. If one of the values is a Float or Double data type, then the result will be a floating-point data type as well.

> **Note** Be careful when dividing two integers since you can't always be sure that the result will be an integer. You will not see the remainder (unless you also use the remainder operator separately). You must explicitly type the receiving variable or constant as a Float or Double (or one of the values being divided must be a floating-point type) to get the floating-point result.

Remainder Operator

When you use the division operator (/), you will get the whole number part only when you are dividing integers. If you want to also use the remainder part of the result, you can use the remainder operator (%).

For example, if you wanted to divide 13 by 3, you could use the code in Listing 14-2.

Listing 14-2. Division and Remainder Operators

```
//Division and remainder operators
let r5 = 13 / 3
let r6 = 13 % 3
```

In Listing 14-2, r5 would equal 4, and r6 would be 1.

Order of Operations and Parentheses

You can have more than one arithmetic operator on a line of code. Each operator requires two values unless the operator is a unary operator (see the "Unary Minus Operator" section). The entire set of values and operators is called an *expression*. Expressions are solved going from left to right, and multiplication and division are performed before addition and subtraction. This is called the *order* of operations. You can change the order of operations by using parentheses, which could create a completely different result. See Listing 14-3 for an example.

Listing 14-3. Changing the Order of Operations

```
let r8:Float = 1 + 2 * 3 - 4 / 5
let r9:Float = (1 + 2) * (3 - 4) / 5
```

In Listing 14-3, r8 equals a value of 6.19999980926514, while r9 equals a value of -0.600000023841858.

Increment and Decrement Operators

The unary increment operator (++) and the unary decrement operator (--)Unary decrement operator (--) increase or decrease the value of a number by 1.

You use unary plus (++) as shown in Listing 14-4.

Listing 14-4. Increment Operator

```
var i1 = 5

++i1
```

In Listing 14-4, ++i1 adds 1 to i1, resulting in a value of 6. You could also use decrement operator (--) to decrease the value of i1 by 1.

You could achieve the same effect by simply writing i1 = i1 + 1, but using the increment operator is easier to write.

The placement of the operator here matters. If you place the ++ or -- before the variable, then the value will be changed first and then returned. If you put the operator after the variable, then the original value will be returned first, and the variable will be incremented or decremented (see Listing 14-5).

Listing 14-5. Increment Operator Placement

```
var i1 = 5

//Returns 5
i1

//Returns 6
++i1

//Returns 6
i1++

//Returns 7
i1
```

As you can see in Listing 14-5, when you increment i1 with the ++ as a suffix, you still get the original value reported. But, when you use i1 on the next line of code, you will get the updated value of 7.

Unary Minus Operator

When you need the negative value of a number, you can simply use the unary minus operator to make a number negative. For instance, if you preferred to make i1 negative, then you could do this: i1 = -i1.

There is also a unary plus operator that just returns the same value.

Compound Operators

Arithmetic operators can be combined with the assignment operator (Chapter 13) when you want to perform an arithmetic function and assign the result to the value in the same line of code (see Listing 14-6).

Listing 14-6. Compound Assignment/Arithmetic Operations

```
//Declare and assign i integer equal to 0
var i = 0

//Add 4 to i and assign result back to i
i+=4

//Multiple i by 2 and assign result back to i
i*=2
```

In Listing 14-6, you start off with an integer i that has a value of 0 and then use compound assignment/arithmetic operations to first add 4 to i and then multiply i by 2. You can use any arithmetic operation like this with the assignment operator.

String Concatenation

The addition operator (+) is also used to add strings (and characters) together (see Listing 14-7).

Listing 14-7. String Concatenation

```
let s1 = "Hello"
let s2 = "World"
let s3 = s1 + " " + s2 + "!"
```

Listing 14-7 outputs "Hello World!"

Chapter 15

Comparison Operators

You use *comparison* operators to compare two values. You can test for equality or whether one value is greater or less than another value.

Table 15-1 describes the comparison operators available in Swift.

Table 15-1. Comparison Operators

Operator	Description
x == y	Equal to
x != y	Not equal to
x > y	Greater than
x >=y	Greater than or equal to
x < y	Less than
x <= y	Less than or equal to
x === y	Two objects are equal
x !== y	Two objects are not equal

Note The last two comparison operators in Table 15-1 (=== and !==) apply only to objects (see Chapter 32). Objects are also known as *instances* in Swift.

Comparison operators return a boolean result that you can store in a boolean variable or constant. See Listing 15-1 for an example.

Listing 15-1. Using Comparison Operators

```
let x = 100

let y = 200

//Returns true
let b1 = x < y

//Returns false
let b2 = x == y
```

Comparison operators are often used with if statements (see Chapter 23) to control program flow.

Chapter 16

Ternary Conditional Operator

You use the *ternary* conditional operator to evaluate a question and then do one of two things based on the result of the question. The ternary conditional operator is written like this: `question ? action1 : action2` (see Listing 16-1).

The question is an expression that returns a boolean `true` or `false`. If the question returns `true`, then the first action takes place. If the question returns `false`, then the second action takes place.

Listing 16-1. Ternary Conditional Operator

```
let a = 5

a == 5 ? "We're good" : "Oops, not quite"
```

In Listing 16-1, the first part of the ternary conditional operator is the statement a `==5`, which is using the equality comparison operator to test to see whether a is equal to 5.

In the next part of Listing 16-1, you have two possible actions that can take place separated by the semicolon (`:`). The first action, "We're good," takes place if the statement is true, while the second action, "Oops, not quite," takes place if the statement is not true.

The ternary conditional operator is a shorthand version of the `if` statement that is covered in more detail in Chapter 23.

Chapter 17

Range Operators

You use *range* operators to specify a range of integers such as 1 through 10. There are two types of range operators: the closed range operator (...) and the half-open range operator (..<).

Closed Range Operator

The closed range operator gives you a way to specify a range of numbers when you want to include the number that defines the end of the range. You must specify the beginning of the range and the end of the range with the closed range operator (...), as shown in Listing 17-1.

Listing 17-1. Closed Range Operator

```
1...10
```

This operator is not useful by itself, but you will see range operators used in for loops (see Chapter 22), as shown in Listing 17-2.

Listing 17-2. Closed Range Operator in a for Loop

```
for i in 1...10 {
    println("i = \(i)")
}
```

The code in Listing 17-2 produces output that includes i = 1 through i = 10 (see Listing 17-3).

Listing 17-3. for Loop Output

```
i = 1
i = 2
i = 3
i = 4
i = 5
i = 6
i = 7
i = 8
i = 9
i = 10
```

Half-Open Range Operator

The half-open range operator (..<) works like the closed range operator except that the ending value in the range is not included. So, if you replaced the closed range operator in the for loop from Listing 17-2 with a half-open range operator, you would print out to i = 9 only (see Listing 17-4).

Listing 17-4. Half-Open Range Operator in for Loop

```
for i in 0..<10 {
    println("i = \(i)")
}
```

The output from the for loop in Listing 17-4 would produce Listing 17-5.

Listing 17-5. for Loop Output

```
i = 0
i = 1
i = 2
i = 3
i = 4
i = 5
i = 6
i = 7
i = 8
i = 9
```

Chapter 18

Logical Operators

The *logical* operators are used with boolean values and expressions that return boolean values. You use these operators to deal with expressions that are made up of parts that can be either true or false. Logical operators are used to test whether two expressions are true or whether one expression is true. Table 18-1 describes the logical operators supported by Swift.

Table 18-1. Logical Operators

Operator	Description
!x	Logical NOT
x && y	Logical AND
x || y	Logical OR

For instance, let's assume you already have two variables, x and y, with values of true and false. To test and see whether both x and y are true, you would use logical AND, as shown in Listing 18-1.

Listing 18-1. Logical AND

```
let x = true
let y = false

let a = x && y
```

In Listing 18-1, the value of a would be false because x and y are not both true.

If you were interested only in whether one condition was true, you could use logical OR to test for this, as shown in Listing 18-2.

Listing 18-2. Logical OR

```
let x = true
let y = false

let b = x || y
```

In Listing 18-2, the value of b would be true because one of the conditions (x) is true.

You use logical NOT as indicated by ! to test for the opposite of a boolean value. An exclamation point before a boolean value means the opposite of the boolean value. So, !true means false, while !false means true.

If you wanted to test x to see what the opposite boolean value is, you could do Listing 18-3.

Listing 18-3. Logical NOT

```
let x = true
let y = false

let c = !x
```

The c value in Listing 18-3 will be false since the value of x is true.

> **Note**   While you can use logical operators by assigning the results to boolean variables or constants, you will most often see logical operators used with if statements (see Chapter 23).

Chapter **19**

Enumerations

You use an enumeration (or an *enum*) to define a restricted set of values. Enums make your code clearer because you can use descriptive names instead of something abstract like an integer value.

If you wanted to define an enumeration to describe a machine state, you could do something like Listing 19-1.

Listing 19-1. Defining Enumerations

```
enum State {
    case Inactive
    case Active
    case Hibernate
    case Terminated
}

var machineState = State.Inactive
```

In Listing 19-1, you defined an enum named State that can have four values: Inactive, Active, Hibernate, and Terminated. You specify enum values with the case keyword. You can specify one value per case keyword, or you can provide a comma-separated list of enum values on one line.

You can use enumeration types like other types. In Listing 19-1, you are assigning the value State.Inactive to the variable machineState.

You can also reference the enum type in the ternary conditional operator (Chapter 16), if statements (Chapter 23), switch statements (Chapter 24), and anywhere else variables or constants are used.

Listing 19-2 shows an example of how you would use the State enum with the ternary conditional operator.

Listing 19-2. Using Enums

```
machineState == State.Inactive ?  println("Machine Inactive") :
println("Machine State Unknown")
```

In Listing 19-2, the text "Machine Inactive" will appear since the value of machineState is State.Inactive.

Enum types can be defined as their own value types, or you can assign other types to an enumeration, including integers, strings, and floating-point numbers.

To assign another type to an enumeration, you must specify the enum type and then use the assignment operator to assign the values. For instance, if you wanted to define an enumeration for the alphabet while keeping track of the position of each letter in the alphabet, you could use the code in Listing 19-3.

Listing 19-3. Integer Enum

```
enum Alphabet:Int{
    case A = 1
    case B, C, D, E, F, G, H, I
    case J, K, L, M, N, O, P, Q
    case R, S, T, U, V, W, X, Y, Z
}
```

In Listing 19-3, you defined the enum type Alphabet as an Int. This means each Alphabet value has a corresponding integer value. You also need to provide each enum value with a corresponding integer value. You did this for case A, which has a value of 1. Since this is an integer type, Swift can figure out that you want the remaining enum values to correspond to integer values in the order you listed them.

While you would use Alphabet in the same way as State, with Alphabet you can reference the raw integer value using the toRaw() function.

For instance, if you want to add the integer value of A to the integer value of B, you would use the code in Listing 19-4.

Listing 19-4. Accessing Raw Enum Values

```
let result = Alphabet.A.toRaw() + Alphabet.B.toRaw()
```

toRaw() is a function. See Chapter 27 for a detailed example of Swift functions.

Chapter **20**

Arrays

To organize a list of variables, constants, and other types, you can use arrays. All items in an array must be of the same type, and you can have lists of items such as integers, floating-point numbers, strings, and objects. Listing 20-1 shows two ways to create empty arrays that you can add items to later.

Listing 20-1. Creating Arrays

```
var a1:Array<String> = Array<String>()
var a2:[String] = [String]()
```

The first line in Listing 20-1 shows you the long way of declaring an array. You must use the `Array` keyword and include the type that is stored in the array between the less-than (<) and greater-than (>) signs. In Listing 20-1, a1 is an array that can hold a list of strings.

You must also use the assignment operator (=) to initialize the array followed by the word `Array` along with the type between the less-than (<) and greater-than (>) signs. You can see two parentheses after the type in the first line of code in Listing 20-1, which is a call to the default initializer. This initializer creates the array object.

There is also a shorthand method for creating arrays, and that is how you create the a2 array shown in Listing 20-1. a2 simply has the type in square brackets: `[String]`.

When you have items that you want in the array when you initially create the array, you can make the array declaration even simpler. This is because Swift supports type inference, and you can omit the initialization and the type declaration (see Listing 20-2).

Listing 20-2. Array Type Inference

```
var a3 = ["A", "B", "C"]
```

In Listing 20-2, you simply set a3 to ["A", "B", "C"], which was enough information for Swift to figure out that a3 is a String array. ["A", "B", "C"] is known as an *array literal*, which is a quick way to write out a constant array.

Array Mutability

Since both of the arrays in Listing 20-1 are declared with the var keyword, they are considered *mutable*. This means you can add, remove, and change the items in the list. You can also use immutable arrays if you use the let keyword when creating the array (see Listing 20-3).

Listing 20-3. Immutable Array Example

```
let ma1 = ["D", "E", "F"]

//Causes build error
ma1+="G"
```

In Listing 20-3, you can see an example of using the let keyword to create an immutable array. Immutable arrays cannot be changed, and if you attempt to add a new item to the array, you will get a build error.

Adding Items to Arrays

Arrays store items in a list that is indexed by integers starting with zero. Use the += operator or the append function to add items to the end of an array (see Listing 20-4).

Listing 20-4. Adding Items

```
a1+="Apples"
a1.append("Oranges")
```

a1 would now contain the two strings "Apples" and "Oranges". If you want to add a new item to the array but you don't want the item to be appended to the end of the list, you can use the insert function, as shown in Listing 20-5.

Listing 20-5. Inserting Items

```
a1.insert("Pineapples", atIndex: 1)
```

When you add the code from Listing 20-5, your list will look like this: [Apples, Pineapples, Oranges]. Type a1 into your playground to see this for yourself.

Removing Items from Arrays

To remove items from arrays, you use removeAtIndex(). All you need to do is supply the index of the item you want to remove from the array. Listing 20-6 shows an example of that function along with some others that you can use to remove items from arrays.

Listing 20-6. Removing Items

```
a1.removeAtIndex(0)

a1.removeLast()

a1.removeAll(keepCapacity: false)
```

In Listing 20-6, you removed the first item from a1 using the removeAtIndex() function and then removed the last item using the function removeLast(). Finally, you removed all remaining items with the function removeAll(keepCapacity:). The parameter in removeAll(keepCapacity:) lets you indicate whether you want the array to stay initialized for the number of items that the array contained. If you know you are replacing the items immediately, it could save processing resources if you leave the array initialized.

Changing Items in Arrays

To change an item in an array, you simply reference the item index in square brackets and use the assignment operator to change the item (see Listing 20-7).

Listing 20-7. Changing Array Items

```
var a4 = [1, 2, 33, 4, 5]

a4[2] = 3
```

In Listing 20-7, you start with an array of integers based on this array literal: [1, 2, 33, 4, 5]. Then, you change the number 33 in the third position to 3.

In Listing 20-7, you can see an example of how to access an array value using the integer index. You include the index of the item in square brackets after the array name to access an item in an array. You access the third value (written as 2 because the array index starts at 0) of array a4.

Iterating Over Array Items

When you have a list of items stored in an array, there are many situations where you want to be able to go over each item in the array and access the item's value or perform some action on the item. You can use the `for-in` loop to do this (see Listing 20-8).

Listing 20-8. Array Iteration

```
for i in a4{
    println("i = \(i)")
}
```

Listing 20-8 used a `for-in` loop to iterate over each item in the a4 array. Each item value will be accessed and printed out to the console log. Loops are covered in more detail in Chapter 22. Here is what the loop in Listing 20-8 will print out to the log:

```
i = 1
i = 2
i = 3
i = 4
i = 5
```

Chapter 21

Dictionaries

Use a dictionary when you want to store items that you need to reference with unique identifier keys. Arrays keep items in the order in which you put the items into the array, while dictionaries don't guarantee any order at all. However, you can access each item based on the key that you provided when the item was originally added to the dictionary.

To create a new dictionary, you will need to specify both the data type for the key and the data type for the value (see Listing 21-1).

Listing 21-1. Declaring Dictionaries

```
var d1:Dictionary<String, Int>
```

In Listing 21-1, d1 is declared as a dictionary that requires String keys and Int values. Before you add any items, you will need to initialize d1 (see Listing 21-2).

Listing 21-2. Initializing Dictionaries

```
d1 = Dictionary()
```

Oftentimes, you will declare the dictionary and initialize the dictionary with a dictionary literal (see Listing 21-3). A dictionary literal is an constant dictionary that is filled with an immutable collection of keys and values.

Listing 21-3. Dictionary Literals

```
var webPages = [1:"http://site/home", 2:"http://site/blog",
3:"http://site/contact"]
```

The code in Listing 21-3 creates a dictionary called webPages that uses integers as keys and stores web page addresses as string values.

Referencing Dictionary Items

To reference a dictionary item, you must supply the key enclosed in square brackets, [ ], after the dictionary name (see Listing 21-4).

Listing 21-4. Referencing Dictionary Items

```
var webPages = [1:"http://site/home", 2:"http://site/blog",
3:"http://site/contact"]

let blogPage = webPages[2]
```

In Listing 21-4, the constant blogPage will be set to http://site/blog since the integer key value 2 points to the string http://site/blog.

Updating Dictionary Items

You can update the value of a mutable dictionary by getting a reference to the item and using the assignment operator to supply the new value (see Listing 21-5).

Listing 21-5. Updating Dictionary Items

```
webPages[1] = "http://site/home/a"
```

In Listing 21-5, you simply provide the key in square brackets to change the web page address. This works the same way for other kinds of keys such as strings and floating-point numbers (see Listing 21-6).

Listing 21-6. Using String and Float Keys

```
var d2:Dictionary = ["a":"AAAA", "b":"BBBB"]
var d3:Dictionary = [1.1:"AAAA", 1.2:"BBBB"]

d2["a"] = "AAAAaaaa"
d3[1.2] = "BBBBbbbb"
```

The code in Listing 21-6 uses String keys to access and change d2 dictionary values. It also uses floating-point numbers to reference and change d3 dictionary values.

To remove an item from a dictionary, simply update the item with the nil value or use the removeValueForKey() function (see Listing 21-7).

Listing 21-7. Removing Items

```
d2["b"] = nil
d2.removeValueForKey("a")
```

In Listing 21-7, you use the `removeValueForKey()` function to remove the value for key a from dictionary d2.

Iterating Over Dictionary Items

To iterate over dictionary items, use the `for-in` loop (see Chapter 22 for more information on loops). You will get a reference to each key and item in the loop (see Listing 21-8).

Listing 21-8. Iterating Over Dictionary Items

```
for (key, value) in d3{
    println("key:\(key), value:\(value)")
}
```

The loop in Listing 21-8 prints this:

```
key:1.10000002384186, value:AAAA
key:1.20000004768372, value:BBBBbbbb
```

If you only need to iterate through the keys, you can access the key property on the dictionary, as shown in Listing 21-9.

Listing 21-9. Iterating Over Dictionary Keys

```
for key in d3.keys{
    println("key:\(key)")
}
```

Listing 21-9 will print out the keys like this:

```
key:1.10000002384186
key:1.20000004768372
```

Chapter 22

Loops

When you want to repeat operations, you can use loops. Loops give you a neat way to do something a set number of times or to do operations until a certain condition (that you define) is met. Collection types such as arrays and dictionaries use loops for iteration.

for-condition-increment Loop

This for loop will be familiar to many programmers. The for-condition-increment loop gives you a loop that will execute a set number of times. You will have to use the for keyword along with an ending condition and an increment statement.

The loop shown in Listing 22-1 prints out 1 through 10 to the console as an example.

Listing 22-1. for-condition-increment Loop

```
for var i - 1; i <- 10; ++i {
    println("i = \(i)")
}
```

Let's look at the loop in Listing 22-1 more closely. The first thing you see is the for keyword. This indicates you are using a for loop. Next you can see three sections of code separated by semicolons (;).

The first section of code, var i = 1, declares a variable i and then assigns 1 to the variable i.

The next section of code is i <= 10;. This is the condition part of the for-condition-increment loop. This means the loop will execute as long as the value of i is less than or equal to 10.

Next, you have the increment part of the for-condition-increment loop: ++i;. This means i will increment by 1 each time the loop executes.

Finally, you have the code block between the curly brackets, {}, and the code that you want to execute in the loop: println("i = \(i)").

When the loop from Listing 22-1 executes, the following list is printed out to the console:

```
i = 1
i = 2
i = 3
i = 4
i = 5
i = 6
i = 7
i = 8
i = 9
i = 10
```

for-in Loop

Use the for-in loop to iterate over items in collections such as arrays and dictionaries. To use a for-in loop, you must specify a local variable name and the collection you are iterating over. Like other for loops, you also need to supply the for keyword and put the code that executes each time into a code block.

Listing 22-2. for-in Loops

```
let names = ["Jim", "John", "Jill"]

for n in names{
    println(n)
}

let inventory = [1:"TV", 2:"Bookcase", 3:"Table"]

for (key,item) in inventory{
    println("\(key) : \(item)")
}
```

In Listing 22-2 you use for-in loops to iterate through the array names and the dictionary inventory and print out the items in each collection.

You can also iterate through a range specified by a range operator (see Chapter 17), as shown in Listing 22-3.

Listing 22-3. Iterating with Range Operators

```
var result = 0

for i in 1...3{
    ++result
}

result
```

The code in Listing 22-3 uses a range operator to specify a range between 1 and 3 and uses this to increment the variable result.

While Loop

while loops work by evaluating a condition and executing code as long as the condition is true. You write a while loop by including the while keyword followed by the condition and the code block to execute (see Listing 22-4).

Listing 22-4. while Loop

```
var i = 1

while i <= 10{
    println("i = \(i)")
    i++
}
```

In Listing 22-4 you reformulated the for-condition-increment loop from Listing 22-1 as a while loop to get the same result.

```
i = 1
i = 2
i = 3
i = 4
i = 5
i = 6
i = 7
i = 8
i = 9
i = 10
```

do-while Loop

The do-while loop will execute the code in the block before evaluating the condition. Use this loop when you want to make sure that code executes at least one time. Listing 22-5 shows how you would rewrite the while loop from Listing 22-4 as a do-while loop.

Listing 22-5. do-while Loop

```
do{
    println("i = \(i)")
    i++
}while i <= 10
```

The do-while loop in Listing 22-5 required the do keyword followed by a code block. The condition was specified right after the while keyword.

You may have noticed that you just reused the variable i from the while loop in Listing 22-4 and the value of i is already 11. Of course, I'm assuming that you followed along with the code in the order it's presented in this chapter. The do-while loop goes through the code even though the condition was never met, resulting in the following output:

```
i = 11
```

Chapter 23

if Statements

if statements are used when you want to make a choice to execute code based on the result of a comparison expression. To make this work, you evaluate an expression that uses comparison and logical operators to yield a true or false result. If you evaluate an expression to be true, then you can execute the code; otherwise, you can ignore the code.

You need the if keyword and an expression along with a code block to use the if statement (see Listing 23-1).

Listing 23-1. if Statement

```
if (1 < 2){
    println("This is true")
}
```

The statement is saying that if 1 is less than 2, then execute the code that will print out the string "That is true" to the console log.

else Keyword

You can also define an alternate action with the else keyword. This gives you a way of executing either one of two actions based on the results of the expression that you are evaluating (see Listing 23-2).

Listing 23-2. else Keyword

```
if (1 < 2){
    println("That is true")
} else {
    println("Not true")
}
```

Listing 23-2 will print out the text "That is true" to the console log since 1 is always less than 2.

Each if statement can contain nested if statements. This gives you a way of testing multiple conditions. Generally speaking, it's best to limit yourself to three nested if statements at most. Listing 23-3 shows what a nested if statement looks like.

Listing 23-3. Nested if Statements

```
if (1 > 2){
    println("True")
} else {
    if (3 > 4){
        println("True")
    } else {
        println("Not True")
    }
}
```

The code from Listing 23-3 will print out "Not True" to the console log.

Chapter 24

switch Statements

switch statements are used to execute code based on the value of a variable. To make a switch statement work, you need to define a level variable, and then you need to write a code block for each possible value of the level variable that you expect.

For this chapter, let's assume you are writing code to help you do some geometry work. You have different shapes that you need to work with, and you want to calculate the area of each shape. You can keep track of what type of shape you are working with by using an integer variable named shape (see Listing 24-1).

Listing 24-1. shape Variable

```
var shape = 0
```

Each value of shape will correspond to a type of shape; for instance, 0 could be a square, 1 could be a parallelogram, and 2 could be a circle. Variables like shape are called *level* variables because they represent possible levels.

For the purposes of this example, you also need a variable to store the results of any calculation you make, which is why you define a float variable named area (see Listing 24-2).

Listing 24-2. area Variable

```
var area: Float?
```

In Listing 24-2, you define area as an optional float to accommodate situations where the shape you are looking at is not defined and you need to set the value of area to nil.

switch Keyword

Now, let's get to the switch statement itself. To start a switch statement, you need the switch keyword followed by the level variable. Use curly braces to create a code block for the switch statement (see Listing 24-3).

Listing 24-3. switch Statement

```
switch shape {

}
```

Case Keyword

Next, you can define code that will be associated with each value that the level variable can take on. You use the case keyword to associate each possible value with a code block (see Listing 24-4).

Listing 24-4. Completed switch Statement

```
switch shape {

case 0:
    let length: Float = 3
    area = length * length
    println("Square area is \(area!)")

default:
    area = nil
    println("No Shape Specified")

}
```

What you see in Listing 24-4 is the case keyword followed by the value that you are testing for, which is 0. Then you have a colon. The code after the colon will execute when the value of shape is 0.

If you look at Listing 24-4, you can see that there is a default keyword. This keyword is used to define a default case, which is a way to define a code block that will execute if no other condition is met. So, if the value of shape happened to be 6 and had no code block defined, you would be sure that at least the code that was included in the default case would execute.

Usually, switch statements will include more than one level (see Listing 24-5).

Listing 24-5. Completed switch Statement

```
switch shape {

case 0:
    let length: Float = 3
    area = length * length
    println("Square area is \(area!)")

case 1:
    let base:Float = 16
    let height:Float = 24
    area = base * height
    println("Parallelogram area is \(area!)")

default:
    area = nil
    println("No Shape Specified")

}
```

Here is what you will find in the console log if you run the code from Listing 24-5 when the value of shape is 0:

```
Square area is 9.0
```

If you were to change the value of shape to 1, then the outcome would be different (see Listing 24-6).

Listing 24-6. Selecting Parallelogram

```
shape = 1

switch shape {

case 0:
    let length: Float = 3
    area = length * length
    println("Square area is \(area!)")

case 1:
    let base:Float = 16
    let height:Float = 24
    area = base * height
    println("Parallelogram area is \(area!)")
```

```
default:
    area = nil
    println("No Shape Specified")

}
```

In this instance, the output from Listing 24-6 would be as follows:

```
Parallelogram area is 384.0
```

Chapter 25

Control Transfer Statements

Control transfer statements change the order that your code is executed in. You use these when you have specific situations where you would like to change the normal execution of code based on a condition that you specify. You have four control transfer statements available to you: continue, break, fallthrough, and return.

> **Note** Only the first three control statements are discussed in this chapter because the return control statement is discussed in Chapter 27.

continue Statement

Use the continue statement with loops to stop code execution and return to the beginning of the loop's code block. For example, let's say you wanted to print out the numbers 1 through 3 and 8 through 10 to the console log screen. You could do something like Listing 25-1.

Listing 25-1. continue Statement

```
for i in 1...10 {
    if (i >=4 && i <= 7){
        continue
    }
    println(i)
}
```

In Listing 25-1, you use the range operator 1...10 to specify a for loop that will execute the code block 10 times. You also have an if statement in the for loop's code block that tests to see whether i is between the values of 4 and 7. When the if statement is true, you use the continue keyword to stop executing the current block. Then you go back to the beginning. The output produced by the code from Listing 25-1 will look like this:

```
1
2
3
8
9
10
```

The numbers 4 through 7 are not printed because of the continue statement.

break Statement

A break statement completely interrupts the execution of a loop. If you replaced the continue statement with the break statement in the loop from Listing 25-1, the output would look much different (see Listing 25-2).

Listing 25-2. break Statement

```
for i in 1...10 {
    if (i >=4 && i <= 7){
        break
    }
    println(i)
}
```

The loop from Listing 25-2 will stop executing completely once the condition i == 4 is true. The output from Listing 25-2 will look like this:

```
1
2
3
```

You can use break statements in switch statements. break statements work in the same way for switch statements as they do for loops; when the break statement is reached, program control leaves the switch statement and resumes at the end right after the ending curly brace, }, as shown in Listing 25-3.

Listing 25-3. Break in switch Statement

```
let x = 6

switch x {

case 0...5:
    println("0 through 5")

case 6:
    break

case 7:
    println("Value 7")

default:
    println("Default")

}
```

Listing 25-3 will print "0 through 5," "Value 7," or "Default" depending on the value of x except when x is equal to 6. When x equals 6, nothing happens at all. In this way, you use break to code exceptions with switch statements.

fallthrough Statement

In C programming, switch statements will automatically fall through to the next case statement if you don't include break statements after each case statement. Swift doesn't behave in this way. When a case condition is made, code execution stops in the switch and resumes right after the ending curly bracket, }.

If you would like to code switch statements that do include this fall-through behavior, you can use the fallthrough statement.

If you changed the switch statement from Listing 25-3 to make the code implement fall-through behavior instead of break behavior, you could do what's shown in Listing 25-4.

Listing 25-4. fallthrough Statement

```
switch x {

case 0...5:
    println("0 through 5")

case 6:
    fallthrough
```

```
case 7:
    println("Value 6 or 7")

default:
    println("Default")

}
```

In Listing 25-4, when x is equal to six, control will fall through to case 7, and the output "Value 6 or 7" will be printed.

Chapter 26

Labeled Statements

Sometimes your programs can become complicated when you start to nest control structures such as loops, `if` statements, and `switch` statements. With Swift, you can label control statements and then use control transfer statements (Chapter 25). You can use the `break`, `continue`, and `fallthrough` control statements with labeled statements.

For instance, let's assume you have two nested loops to print integers from 1 to 3, as shown in Listing 26-1.

Listing 26-1. Nested Loop

```
for x in 1...3 {
    for y in 1...3 {
        println("x = \(x), y = \(y)")
    }
}
```

The code from Listing 26-1 will print out this:

```
x = 1, y = 1
x = 1, y = 2
x = 1, y = 3
x = 2, y = 1
x = 2, y = 2
x = 2, y = 3
x = 3, y = 1
x = 3, y = 2
x = 3, y = 3
```

If you wanted to skip any value where y equals 2, you could just include a continue statement right inside the innermost loop (see Listing 26-2).

Listing 26-2. continue Statement

```
for x in 1...3 {
    for y in 1...3 {
        if y == 2{
            continue
        }
        println("x = \(x), y = \(y)")
    }
}
```

Here you are skipping those situations where y is 2 because of the continue statement, which brings control back to the beginning of the innermost loop.

The output from Listing 26-2 will look like this:

```
x = 1, y = 1
x = 1, y = 3
x = 2, y = 1
x = 2, y = 3
x = 3, y = 1
x = 3, y = 3
```

If your intention is to skip all the way back to the outermost loop, you will be out of luck with this approach unless you use a label statement. You can label each loop first as shown in Listing 26-3.

Listing 26-3. Labeled Statements

```
outerloop: for x in 1...3 {
    innerloop: for y in 1...3 {
        if y == 2{
            continue
        }
        println("x = \(x), y = \(y)")
    }
}
```

Once you label the statements, you can choose which labeled statement to apply the control transfer statement to (see Listing 26-4).

Listing 26-4. Labeled continue Statement

```
outerloop: for x in 1...3 {
    innerloop: for y in 1...3 {
        if y == 2{
            continue outerloop
        }
        println("x = \(x), y = \(y)")
    }
}
```

In Listing 26-4, you are still testing to see when y is equal to 2. When this situation is true, you send control all the way back to the outer loop. This results in output like this:

```
x = 1, y = 1
x = 2, y = 1
x = 3, y = 1
```

As you can see, this changes the output dramatically. Labeled statements give you much more control and clarity when you are dealing with complex and nested control structures.

Chapter **27**

Functions

You can declare a function anywhere with the func keyword. Functions are used to organize code into reusable chunks that take input parameters and return results. Listing 27-1 shows an example of a function that returns the string "Hello World."

Listing 27-1. Simple Function

```
func getPhrase() -> String{
    return "Hello World"
}
```

In Listing 27-1, the function declaration starts with the func keyword followed by the name of the function. After the function name in Listing 27-1, you have (), which designates an empty parameter list. The return type of the function (String) is written after the return type symbol ->.

After the function return type, you have a code block designated in the curly brackets, {}. The getPhrase() function has only one line of code, which simply returns a string to the caller. The return keyword is a control transfer statement that returns code execution to the caller.

To call the function, just use the name of the function including the parameter values in parentheses. In the case of the function declared in Listing 27-1, you can call the function as shown in Listing 27-2.

Listing 27-2. Calling Functions

```
let s = getPhrase();

println(s)
```

As you can see, you call the function and assign the results to a constant and then print that to the log. Usually, you will assign results of functions to variables or constants, but you could have also used the getPhrase() function directly with the println(), as shown in Listing 27-3.

Listing 27-3. Calling Functions Directly

```
println(getPhrase())
```

Not all functions return results. Listing 27-4 shows an example of a function that just writes out the log without returning a value.

Listing 27-4. Void Function

```
func justDoSomething() {

    println("Printing justDoSomething() function")

    return
}
```

Functions like the one declared in Listing 27-4 are sometimes called *void* functions. To call this function, you can simply type the name of the function followed by the empty parentheses, as shown in Listing 27-5.

Listing 27-5. Calling Void Functions

```
justDoSomething()
```

Parameters

To declare a function with parameters, you include the name of the parameter and the data type of the parameter (see Listing 27-6).

Listing 27-6. Declaring Parameters

```
func averageScore(scores:[Float]) -> Float{

    var total:Float = 0
    var count:Float = 0

    for score in scores{
        total+=score
        count++
    }

    return total / count
}
```

In Listing 27-6, you declared a function named averageScore that takes an array of Float values as a parameter. The function will return a Float value. In the code block, you add all the scores together and divide by the number of scores in the array. That value is returned to the caller.

Listing 27-7 shows how you would call this function.

Listing 27-7. Calling Functions with Parameters

```
let result = averageScore([0, 90, 84, 76, 67, 95, 73, 89])
```

In Listing 27-7, you called the function with an array literal that defined a range of scores. Listing 27-7 would output the result 71.75.

When functions have more than one parameter, you include them in a comma-separated list, as shown in Listing 27-8.

Listing 27-8. Multiple Parameters

```
func printStuff (this:String, that:String){

    println("\(this) \(that)!")

    return
}

printStuff("Hello", "World")
```

In Listing 27-8, you defined a function that prints out the two strings that you supplied in the function call to the console log. When you call printStuff like in Listing 27-8, you will get the "Hello World!" message printed out.

Chapter 28

Nested Functions

You can code functions within other functions. *Nesting* functions gives you a way to organize and reuse your code while limiting the scope of functions to the parent function.

For instance, let's say you wanted to write a Swift program to help a teacher summarize how some students performed on the tests they took this week. You could write a function called `analyzeTestScores()` that would figure out what the average score of a test was including all students and then would write a report.

Since this function has to do a few things, it makes sense to organize each task into separate functions. You could start by adding a function that returns the average test score based on an array of numbers (see Listing 28-1).

Listing 28-1. Nested Functions

```
func analyzeTestScores(){

    func averageScore(scores:[Int]) -> Float?{
        if scores.count > 0 {
            var total:Int = 0
            var count:Int = 0
            for score in scores{
                total+=score
                count++
            }
            return (Float)(total / count)
        }
        else {
            return nil
        }
    }

}
```

In Listing 28-1, you start your analysis by declaring the function averageScore([Int]) inside the function analyzeTestScores(). This means that code located in analyzeTestScores() can now use this function. averageScore([Int]) will take an array of integers and return a Float value representing the average test score or nil.

Your analysis would include a report as well, so you would want to add another nested function to analyzeTestScores(), as shown in Listing 28-2.

Listing 28-2. Calling Nested Functions

```
func analyzeTestScores(){

    func averageScore(scores:[Int]) -> Float?{
        if scores.count > 0 {
            var total:Int = 0
            var count:Int = 0
            for score in scores{
                total+=score
                count++
            }
            return (Float)(total / count)
        }
        else {
            return nil
        }
    }

    func printReport(testName:String, scores:[Int]){
        if let a = averageScore(scores){
            println("\(testName) Test Results")
            println(" The average score is \(a)")
        }
    }

}
```

In Listing 28-2, the function printReport(String, [Int]) takes a list of test scores as a parameter along with a String parameter that you can use for the test name. This function will call the averageScore([Int]) function right in the optional binding statement using the array of test scores as a parameter. Finally, the test name and average score will be printed to the log.

To get this analysis started, you will need to call these functions from within analyzeTestScores(), as shown in Listing 28-3.

Listing 28-3. Calling Nested Functions

```
func analyzeTestScores(){

    func averageScore(scores:[Int]) -> Float?{
        if scores.count > 0 {
            var total:Int = 0
            var count:Int = 0
            for score in scores{
                total+=score
                count++
            }
            return (Float)(total / count)
        }
        else {
            return nil
        }
    }

    func printReport(testName:String, scores:[Int]){
        if let a = averageScore(scores){
            println("\(testName) Test Results")
            println(" The average score is \(a)")
        }
    }

    printReport("Math", [90, 84, 76, 67, 45, 95, 73, 89])
    printReport("Social Studies", [36, 17, 42, 25])

}
```

In Listing 28-3, you call printReport(String, [Int]) two times. Each time you supply a different set of test scores and a different test name. To finally get all this to run, you must run the topmost function analyzeTestScores() from the main part of the playground (see Listing 28-4).

Listing 28-4. Calling Nested Functions

```
func analyzeTestScores(){

    func averageScore(scores:[Int]) -> Float?{
        if scores.count > 0 {
            var total:Int = 0
            var count:Int = 0
            for score in scores{
                total+=score
                count++
            }
            return (Float)(total / count)
        }
```

```
        else {
            return nil
        }
    }

    func printReport(testName:String, scores:[Int]){
        if let a = averageScore(scores){
            println("\(testName) Test Results")
            println(" The average score is \(a)")
        }
    }

    printReport("Math", [90, 84, 76, 67, 45, 95, 73, 89])
    printReport("Social Studies", [36, 17, 42, 25])

}

analyzeTestScores()
```

Nested functions are one construct that you have available to you in Swift to keep your code organized and reusable.

> **Note**   Variables in functions are scoped in the same way as other types in Swift. Variables can be used in the functions they are declared in and in any nested function.

The code from Listing 28-4 will result in the following output:

```
Math Test Results
 The average score is 77.0
Social Studies Test Results
 The average score is 30.0
```

Chapter 29

Chapter **29**

Closures

Closures are blocks of code that you can pass to functions as parameters or store as variables or constants to be used later. Closures capture the state of the other variables around them. These constructs are often used when you want to perform operations that don't need to happen immediately but depend on local state. Closures are also used frequently with functions to give callers a way of adding behavior to a function that would normally be out of scope.

One example of where closures are used is as an argument to the Swift standard library sorted function. This function takes an array and a closure as parameters. The array contains the items that need to be sorted, and the closure includes the instructions that will be used to sort the items (see Listing 29-1).

Listing 29-1. Sorted Function

```
var alpha = ["D", "E", "A", "C", "B"]

let alpha_sorted = sorted(alpha, { (s1: String, s2: String) -> Bool in
    return s1 < s2
})
```

In Listing 29-1, you can see the closure highlighted. The entire code block is enclosed in curly brackets. In the top area you see the closure parameters in parentheses followed by the return type Bool. In contrast to functions, closures require the in keyword before you add the code block.

The items in alpha_sorted would be in the following order:

```
["A", "B", "C", "D", "E"]
```

Closures can be stored in variables or constants and used later as parameters. The code from Listing 29-1 could be rewritten as shown in Listing 29-2.

Listing 29-2. Closure Variables

```
let closure = { (s1: String, s2: String) -> Bool in
    return s1 < s2
};

let alpha_sorted_2 = sorted(alpha, closure)
```

In Listing 29-2, you assign the closure to a constant named closure and then use this constant as the input parameter to the sorted function. You could also use the closure like a function.

The items in alpha_sorted_2 would also be in the following order:

```
["A", "B", "C", "D", "E"]
```

Listing 29-3. Calling Closures

```
let closure = { (s1: String, s2: String) -> Bool in
    return s1 < s2
};

let b = closure("B", "A")
```

In Listing 29-3, b would be false because you used the closure to compare the values "B" and "A", and because B is not less than A, the closure returned false.

Chapter 30

Structures

You can use structures to define custom types in Swift. Structures give you a way of grouping related information together. These Swift constructs give you the same capability as structures in C programming, but as you will see, Swift structures are richer than C structures.

To define a Swift structure, use the `struct` keyword (see Listing 30-1).

Listing 30-1. Defining Custom Types

```
struct Rectangle {
    var x:Int = 0
    var y:Int = 0
    var width:Int = 0
    var height:Int = 0
}
```

In Listing 30-1, you define a structure named `Rectangle`. Your rectangle type is made of integers that describe the rectangle, including the x and y origin coordinates and the `height` and `width` dimensions.

When used like this in structures and classes (Chapter 31), these variable and constant types are called *properties*.

Structure Instances

In Listing 30-1, you defined what a rectangle will look like generally. To use a structure type, you must create a new instance based on this definition (see Listing 30-2).

Listing 30-2. Structure Instances

```
struct Rectangle {
    var x:Int = 0
    var y:Int = 0
    var width:Int = 0
    var height:Int = 0
}

var rect = Rectangle()
```

Accessing Structure Properties

To access structure properties, you use dot syntax (see Listing 30-3).

Listing 30-3. Accessing Properties

```
rect.x = 10
rect.y = 10
rect.width = 100
rect.height = 50

println("x: \(rect.x), y: \(rect.y), width: \(rect.width),
height: \(rect.height)")
```

In the first four lines of Listing 30-3, you use dot syntax to change the variable values to the values you require. In the last line of code in Listing 30-3, you can see an example of properties being used in the print function with dot syntax.

> **Note**   Structures are value types. This means members are copied and not passed by reference when the assignment statement is used. Let's say you used an assignment operator to assign the values in x to another structure y. Any changes made to y will not be reflected in x.

Structure Functions

In contrast to C structures, Swift structure types can have functions as part of their definition. This means Swift structures not only can organize data but can define behavior. To add a function to a structure like the rectangle you defined in Listing 30-2, you could do what's shown in Listing 30-4.

Listing 30-4. Structure Functions

```
struct Rectangle {
    var x:Int = 0
    var y:Int = 0
    var width:Int = 0
    var height:Int = 0

    func description() -> String{
        return ("x: \(x), y: \(y), width: \(width), height: \(height)")
    }

}
```

The function defined in Listing 30-4 returns a String that describes the rectangle. To call this function, you must use dot syntax (see Listing 30-5).

Listing 30-5. Calling Structure Functions

```
println(rect.description())
```

The code from Listing 30-5 will print this to the console log:

```
x: 10, y: 10, width: 100, height: 50
```

Chapter **31**

Classes

Use classes to define types in Swift that you want to use as objects. Like structures, classes give you a way of grouping related information and behavior together.

To define a Swift class, use the class keyword (see Listing 31-1).

Listing 31-1. Defining Classes

```
class Person {
    var name: String = "Name"
    var age:Int = 0

    func profile() -> String {
        return "I'm \(self.name) and I'm \(self.age) years old."
    }

}
```

In Listing 31-1, you defined a class named Person. Your Person class consists of a string for a person's name and an integer for a person's age.

When used like this in structures (Chapter 30) and classes, these variable and constant types are called *properties*.

Class Instances (Objects)

In Listing 31-1, you defined what a person will look like generally. To use a Person instance (or *object*), you must create a new instance based on this definition (see Listing 31-2).

Listing 31-2. Class Instances

```
class Person {
    var name: String = "Name"
    var age:Int = 0

    func profile() -> String {
        return "I'm \(self.name) and I'm \(self.age) years old."
    }

}

var p = Person()
```

> **Note**   In Swift, objects are usually references to instances for both structures and classes.

Accessing Class Properties

As you did with structure properties, for class instance properties you use dot syntax (see Listing 31-3).

Listing 31-3. Accessing Properties

```
p.name = "Matt"
p.age = 40
```

In Listing 31-3, you use dot syntax to change the variable values to the values you require.

> **Note**   Classes are reference types. This means when you use an assignment operator, you assign only a reference to the instance. When changes to a class instance members are made, they will reflected in the instance everywhere in the program.

Class Functions

Class types can have functions as part of their definition. Classes not only can organize data but can define behavior. In Listing 31-1, you already added a function named profile() that returns a description of the person in a friendly format.

See Listing 31-4 for an example of how you might use this function.

Listing 31-4. Calling Class Functions

```
println(p.profile())
```

The code from Listing 31-4 will print this to the console log:

```
I'm Matt and I'm 40 years old.
```

Chapter **32**

Using Instances

In the previous two chapters, you saw how to define classes and structures. Structures and classes are used by creating instances (see Listing 32-1).

Listing 32-1. Class and Structure Instances

```
struct S {
    var i = 1
}

class C {
    var i = 1
}

var s = S()

var c = C()
```

As you can see in Listing 32-1, these constructs are nearly identical, with the exception of the class and struct keywords. You use dot syntax to access properties in the same way with both class and structure instances (see Listing 32-2).

Listing 32-2. Accessing Instance Properties

```
println("s.i = \(s.i)")

println("c.i = \(c.i)")
```

The statements in Listing 32-2 will print this:

```
s.i = 1
c.i = 1
```

Reference vs. Copy

You will see the major difference between referencing and copying instances when you use the assignment operator (=) to reference the instance. When you do this for a structure, you get a copy of the instance. This copy acts independently from the original instance. If you make changes to the copy, they will not be reflected in the original instance.

In contrast, if you use the assignment operator to assign a variable to a class instance when you make changes to the class instance members, the original instance content will also change (see Listing 32-3).

Listing 32-3. Copy vs. Reference

```
var s2 = s

var c2 = c

s2.i = 2

c2.i = 2

println("s.i = \(s.i)")

println("c.i = \(c.i)")
```

In Listing 32-3, you assign the instances to new variables and then use the same code as before to print the i values from the original instances. What you get is this:

```
s.i = 1
c.i = 2
```

As you can see, the original structure member didn't change at all. However, the original class instance member's value changed to be the same value as the i property on c2.

Chapter 33

Class Identity Operators

Since class instances are referenced and not copied when you use the assignment operator, it's common to have many variables in your program referring to the same class instance. This makes it important for you to be able to compare two variables to see whether they point to the same class instance.

Let's say you are working with the Person class introduced in Chapter 31 (see Listing 33-1).

Listing 33-1. Person Instances

```
class Person {
    var name: String = "Name"
    var age:Int = 0

    func profile() -> String {
        return "I'm \(self.name) and I'm \(self.age) years old."
    }

}

var p1 = Person()
p1.name = "Matt"
p1.age = 40

var p2 = Person()
p2.name = "Jill"
p2.age = 25
```

In Listing 33-1, you define a Person class and then created two instances. You will be using these instances to see the two class identity operators in action.

Class Equality Identity Operator

You use the class equality operator (===) to compare two class instances (see Listing 33-2). This operator returns true if the instance variables both point to the same instance.

Listing 33-2. Class Instance Equality Operator

```
var b1 = p2 === p2
var b2 = p1 === p2
```

In Listing 33-2, the b1 would be true since they are both the same instance, while b2 would be false. Let's see how this works when instances have been assigned to new variables (see Listing 33-3).

Listing 33-3. Comparing Instance Variables

```
var v1 = p1
var v2 = p2

var b3 = v1 === p1
//returns true
var b4 = v2 === p2
//returns true
var b5 = v2 === p1
//returns false
var b6 = v1 === p2
//returns false
```

In Listing 33-2, you assign the original class instances to two new variables, v1 and v2. As you can see from Listing 33-2, the instance equality operator can tell when the variables point to the original instances.

Class Inequality Identity Operator

The class instance inequality identity operator (!==) tests to see whether two instances do *not* point to the same instance (see Listing 33-4).

Listing 33-4. Inequality Operator

```
var b7 = p1 !== p1
//returns false
var b8 = v1 !== p1
//returns false
```

In Listing 33-4, you can see that the inequality operator is returning false when two instances are the same.

Chapter **34**

Properties

You use properties to describe attributes of an object. To add a property to an object in Swift, you can add a variable or constant declaration to the type definition.

> **Note** Properties are not limited to class definitions in Swift. Enumerations and structures can also have property declarations.

You have already encountered property declarations in Chapter 31 with the declaration of the Person class (see Listing 34-1).

Listing 34-1. Property Declarations

```
class Person {
    var name: String = "Name"
    var age:Int = 0
    func profile() -> String {
        return "I'm \(self.name) and I'm \(self.age) years old."
    }
}
```

In Listing 34-1, you declared two variables, name and age, with initial values. These types of properties are called *stored properties* because they simply store values.

To access properties, you must create an instance of the class or structure and then use dot syntax (see Listing 34-2).

Listing 34-2. Accessing Properties

```
var p = Person()

p.name = "Matt"
p.age = 40

println("p.name = \(p.name)")
println("p.age = \(p.age)")
```

In Listing 34-2, you use dot syntax to change the variable values to the values that you require. In the last two lines of code from Listing 34-2, you can see an example of properties being used in the print function with dot syntax.

You can have code properties that have a getter and setter in addition to the simple stored properties that you see in Listing 34-1 (see Listing 34-3).

Listing 34-3. Property Getters and Setters

```
class Person {
    var name: String = "Name"
    var age:Int = 0
    private var _lastName:String = ""

    var lastName:String{
    get {
        return _lastName
    }
    set {
        _lastName = newValue
    }
    }

    func profile() -> String {
        return "I'm \(self.name) and I'm \(self.age) years old."
    }

}

var p = Person()

p.name = "Matt"
```

In Listing 34-3, you coded a getter and setter that returned the private variable _lastName. You are using _lastName as the local storage here.

Once you have coded getters and setters, you can use them like the properties that you saw when using dot syntax. See Listing 34-3 for an example of using the setter to assign the value of the name property of the p object to Matt.

> **Note**   The `private` keyword is used to limit the visibility of a variable. When you mark a variable as private, you can access this variable only from code in the same file as the private variable.

Lazy and Computed Properties

The purpose of the properties you have seen so far is to store values. These types of properties are called *stored properties* for that reason. You can also define lazy and computed properties.

Lazy Properties

When a property value will not need to be generated until the first time the property value is used, you can use a *lazy* stored property. This option is used when the property represents a resource that may be expensive to generate and needed in only specific situations.

To make a property a lazy stored property, you use the `lazy` modifier. For instance, Listing 34-4 shows how you would make the name property of the Person class a lazy stored property.

Listing 34-4. Lazy Property

```
class Person {
    lazy var name: String = "Name"
    var age:Int = 0
    private var _lastName:String = ""

    var lastName:String{
    get {
        return _lastName
    }
    set {
        _lastName = newValue
    }
    }
```

```
    func profile() -> String {
        return "I'm \(self.name) and I'm \(self.age) years old."
    }

}

var p = Person()

p.name = "Matt"
p.age = 40
```

In Listing 34-4, you use the lazy keyword to make the name property a lazy stored property. In this situation, the lazy attribute doesn't change your program much. But, if you could imagine that the initial value of the name property was hard to calculate and if the name property was not used often, it may make sense to use this pattern.

Computed Properties

Computed properties take input values and return a new result. Computed properties act more like functions in that they perform an action and produce a result. But, computer properties are used like properties with dot syntax.

For instance, the Person class used in the listings in this chapter has a profile() function that you use to write the profile of the person to the console log. You could change this function into a computed property as shown in Listing 34-5.

Listing 34-5. Computed Properties

```
class Person {
    lazy var name: String = "Name"
    var age:Int = 0
    private var _lastName:String = ""

    var lastName:String{
    get {
        return _lastName
    }
    set {
        _lastName = newValue
    }
    }
```

```
    var profile:String{
    get{
        return "I'm \(self.name) and I'm \(self.age) years old."
    }
    }
}

var p = Person()

p.name = "Matt"
p.age = 40

p.profile
```

In Listing 34-5, you used a custom setter to create a computed property for a profile that took the person's information to return a profile description. As you can see from the last line of the listing, you used dot syntax (without the () that a function would need) to access a computed property value.

Here is the output that would appear in the playground:

```
I'm Matt and I'm 40 years old.
```

Chapter 35

Property Observers

You can observe the state of a property with the willSet and didSet keywords. You can use these in the property declaration to assign an action that will occur when a property is about to change and when a property value just changed. Listing 35-1 shows how you would add an action that prints a message to the console log whenever the age property value is about to change and after the age value has changed.

Listing 35-1. Property Observers

```
class Person {
    var name: String = "Name"
    var age:Int = 0{
    willSet{
        println("age value is about to change to \(newValue)")
    }
    didSet{
        println("age value just changed to \(self.age)")
    }
    }

    func profile() -> String {
        return "I'm \(self.name) and I'm \(self.age) years old."
    }

}
```

You use these observers by including a code block that includes a willSet code block and a didSet code block.

When you change the value of the age property, you will get notifications printed to your console log (see Listing 35-2).

Listing 35-2. Observing Property State

```
var p = Person()
p.age = 40
```

In Listing 35-2, you change the value of age to 40, which prints this to the console log:

```
age value is about to change to 40
age value just changed to 40
```

Chapter 36

Class Type Properties

Type properties belong to a particular type, in contrast to the properties discussed in Chapter 34, which belong to instances of a type. You use type properties when you want to have properties that are universal to all instances of that type.

You use the `class` keyword to declare a type property for a class (see Listing 36-1).

Listing 36-1. Declaring Class Type Properties

```
class Person {
    class var species:String{
        return "Homo sapiens"
    }
    var name: String = "Name"
    var age:Int = 0

    func profile() -> String {
        return "I'm \(self.name) and I'm \(self.age) years old."
    }

}
```

In Listing 36-1, you used the `class` keyword to define the type property `species`. Type properties for classes must be computed properties, which is why the return value is enclosed in the curly brackets, {}.

You can access a type property using dot syntax using the class name and the type property. Note that here you don't need to create a new instance to use the type property (see Listing 36-2).

Listing 36-2. Accessing Type Property Values

```
Person.species
```

The code from Listing 36-2 returns the string Homo sapiens. Class type properties are constant.

Value Type Properties

Value type properties can be computed properties or stored properties, and you can change the value of stored type properties. Use the static keyword to declare a type property for an enumeration or a structure (see Listing 36-3).

Listing 36-3. Value Type Properties

```
struct Rectangle {
    var x:Int = 0
    var y:Int = 0
    var width:Int = 0
    var height:Int = 0

    static var gtp = "This describes a rectangle"
}

Rectangle.gtp
```

In Listing 36-2, you use the static keyword to declare a type property. Other than the static keyword, this declaration looks just like a typical property declaration.

You access type property values by referencing the type name and using dot syntax to access the value. The last line of code will print the following to the playground screen:

```
This describes a rectangle
```

You can treat type properties for value types such as enumerations and structures in the same way that you do for instance properties. Listing 36-4 shows how you would change the value of gtp.

Listing 36-4. Accessing Value Type Properties

```
Rectangle.gtp = "Something else"

Rectangle.gtp
```

In Listing 36-4, you change the type property gtp to the string "Something else" and then use dot syntax to retrieve the type property value.

Chapter **37**

Type Methods

In Chapter 31, you coded a function for the Person class named profile().
Class functions are also known as *methods*, and in Chapter 31 you coded
an instance method. Instance methods require a type instance.

In contrast, type methods are functions that require the type (class,
enumeration, or structure) to work. To declare a type method for a class,
you must use the class keyword (see Listing 37-1).

Listing 37-1. Declaring Type Methods

```
class Person {
    class var species:String{
        return "Homo sapiens"
    }

    class func printDescription() {
        println("The Person class defines the structure to represent an
                individual of the species \(species).")
    }

    var name: String = "Name"
    var age:Int = 0

    func profile() -> String {
        return "I'm \(self.name) and I'm \(self.age) years old."
    }

}

Person.printDescription()
```

In Listing 37-1, you code a type method named `printDescription()` that prints a brief description for the `Person` class. You would reference the class name `Person` and call the type method `printDescription()`.

When you call the type function in Listing 37-1, you will get the following output:

The Person class defines the structure to represent an individual of the species Homo sapiens.

Type Methods for Value Types

Structures and enumerations work in the same way for type methods except that you substitute the `class` keyword with the `static` keyword. Listing 37-2 shows how you could add a `printDescription()` type method to the `Rectangle` structure you coded in Chapter 30.

Listing 37-2. Structure Type Method

```
struct Rectangle {
    var x:Int = 0
    var y:Int = 0
    var width:Int = 0
    var height:Int = 0

    static var gtp = "This describes a rectangle"

    static func printDescription() {
        println("The Rectangle structure does this: \(gtp).")
    }

}

Rectangle.printDescription()
```

The code from Listing 37-2 will print this message to the console log:

The Rectangle structure does this: This describes a rectangle.

Chapter **38**

Subscripts

When you use arrays (Chapter 20) and dictionaries (Chapter 21), you get an easy way to access the items in these collections with a subscript. A *subscript* is a key that you use to extract a value from a collection. You can add subscript support to your own types.

To add subscript support to the Person class you first coded in Chapter 31, you can write the code in Listing 38-1.

Listing 38-1. Adding Subscript Support

```
class Person {
    var name: String = "Name"
    var age:Int = 0

    func profile() -> String {
        return "I'm \(self.name) and I'm \(self.age) years old."
    }

    private var roles = ["Manager", "Parent", "Runner"]

    subscript(index: Int) -> String {
        get {
            return roles[index]
        }
        set(newValue) {
            self.roles[index] = newValue
        }
    }

}
```

In Listing 38-1, you added an array named roles that stores three possible roles a person may have: Manager, Parent, and Runner. This is the content you will ultimately expose using subscript notation.

In Listing 38-1, you used the subscript keyword followed by input parameters, the return type, and a getter and setter. The getter and setter define the rules you set to access the data you want to expose with the subscripts.

Once you have subscripts defined in your type, you can access the content in your class in the same way that you would in an array (see Listing 38-2).

Listing 38-2. Accessing Values with Subscripts

```
var p = Person()

println(p[1])

p[0] = "Coach"
```

In Listing 38-2, once you create the new Person instance, you can access data by supplying an integer subscript: p[1]. The println(p[1]) code line will print Parent. In the last line of code from Listing 38-2, you changed the value of one of the items to Coach.

Chapter 39

Inheritance

Classes have the ability to inherit methods and properties from a parent class. Inheritance encourages code reuse. Generally, when you inherit a class, you will add custom properties and methods to the new class.

For instance, if you wanted to create a new class to manage the employees in your small business, you may want to inherit your work from the Parent class into a new class called Employee. Listing 39-1 shows how you would do that.

Listing 39-1. Inheriting Person

```
class Person {
    var name: String = "Name"
    var age:Int = 0

    func profile() -> String {
        return "I'm \(self.name) and I'm \(self.age) years old."
    }
}

class Employee: Person {

}
```

In Listing 39-1, your new class Employee is inheriting Person. To indicate what class you are inheriting, add a colon (:) and the name of the class you are inheriting (called the *parent* class).

Usually, you would add more properties and/or methods to the new class (see Listing 39-2).

Listing 39-2. Custom Properties

```
class Employee: Person {
    var employeeNumber = 1234567890
    var hourlyRate = 12.00
}

var e1 = Employee()
```

In Listing 39-2, you added two employee-specific properties to the `Employee` class: employeeNumber and hourlyRate. In the last line of code, you created a new instance for an employee using the `Employee` class (not the `Person` class).

Now you can use all the properties from `Parent` and `Employee` with your e1 instance (see Listing 39-3).

Listing 39-3. Accessing Properties

```
e1.name = "Jim"
e1.age = 18
e1.employeeNumber = 1
e1.hourlyRate = 15.50
```

In Listing 39-3, you set up the data for the first employee in your business.

Chapter 40

Overriding Methods and Properties

When you use inheritance with a class, you can change how the parent class methods and properties behave by *overriding*. When you override a method, an instance will behave differently than its parent instance even though the same method name is used as the function call.

For instance, in Chapter 39 you had two classes. The parent class name Person had a method named profile() that returned a string describing the Person instance. Employee instances also have this method, and they are identical.

> **Note** In the code in Listing 40-1, the code has been modified from the previous chapter to include a property for a person's last name.

Listing 40-1. Person and Employee Classes

```
class Person {
    var name: String = "Name"
    var age:Int = 0

    func profile() -> String {
        return "I'm \(self.name) and I'm \(self.age) years old."
    }
}
```

```
    private var _lastName:String = ""

    var lastName:String{
    get {
        return _lastName
    }
    set {
        _lastName = newValue
    }
    }

}

class Employee: Person {
    var employeeNumber = 1234567890
    var hourlyRate = 12.00

}

var p1 = Person()

p1.name = "Matt"
p1.lastName = "Campbell"
p1.age = 40

println(p1.profile())

var e1 = Employee()

e1.name = "Jim"
e1.lastName = "Smith"
e1.age = 18
e1.employeeNumber = 1
e1.hourlyRate = 15.50

println(e1.profile())
```

In Listing 40-1, you created two instances: p1, which is a Person instance, and e1, which is an Employee instance. When you print the profile() to the console log, the results are the same (with the exception of the property values) for both instances:

```
I'm Matt and I'm 40 years old.
I'm Jim and I'm 18 years old.
```

You can override the method profile() on the Employee class if you want employees to have a different profile template than other people (see Listing 40-2).

Listing 40-2. Overriding Methods

```
class Employee: Person {
    var employeeNumber = 1234567890
    var hourlyRate = 12.00

    override func profile() -> String {
        return "I'm \(self.name) and my hourly rate is $\(self.hourlyRate)"
    }

}

var p1 = Person()

p1.name = "Matt"
p1.lastName = "Campbell"
p1.age = 40

println(p1.profile())

var c1 = Employee()

e1.name = "Jim"
e1.lastName = "Smith"
e1.age = 18
e1.employeeNumber = 1
e1.hourlyRate = 15.55

println(e1.profile())
```

In Listing 40-2, you used the override keyword to override the method named profile() and change the returned string. Now the output would look like this:

```
I'm Matt and I'm 40 years old.
I'm Jim and my hourly rate is $15.55
```

You can also override property declarations. For instance, if you wanted to keep your employee's last name anonymous, you could override the getter in the Employee class definition. The new getter could return the string Anonymous instead of the employee's real last name (see Listing 40-3).

Listing 40-3. Overriding Properties

```
class Employee: Person {
    var employeeNumber = 1234567890
    var hourlyRate = 12.00

    override func profile() -> String {
        return "I'm \(self.name) and my hourly rate is $\(self.hourlyRate)"
    }
```

```
    override var lastName:String {
    get {
        return "Anonymous"
    }
    set {
        _lastName = newValue
    }
    }

}

var p1 = Person()
p1.lastName = "Campbell"

var e1 = Employee()
e1.lastName = "Smith"

println(p1.lastName)
println(e1.lastName)
```

In Listing 40-3, you used the override keyword to override the lastName property. You can still set the value, but when you attempt to retrieve the value Employee, instances will always return Anonymous. The output from Listing 40-3 would look like this:

```
Campbell
Anonymous
```

Chapter 41

Initialization

You initialize an instance to get the instance ready for use. Initialization means you set the starting values for the instance. In Chapter 31, you used the default initializer when you created a new Person instance (see Listing 41-1).

Listing 41-1. Default Initializer

```
class Person {
    var name: String = "Name"
    var age:Int = 0

    func profile() -> String {
        return "I'm \(self.name) and I'm \(self.age) years old."
    }

}

var p = Person()

p.name = "Matt"
p.age = 40
```

In Listing 41-1, you called the default initializer by using the class name followed by parentheses: Person(). Since you supplied default values for the two properties name and age, this worked fine.

Use init() to override the default initializer. This can be used as an alternative to setting the default property values in the class declaration (see Listing 41-2).

Listing 41-2. Default Initializer

```
class Person {
    var name: String
    var age:Int

    func profile() -> String {
        return "I'm \(self.name) and I'm \(self.age) years old."
    }

    init() {
        self.name = "Name"
        self.age = 0
    }

}
```

In Listing 41-2, you overrode the default initializer init() to set the default property of name to Name and of age to 0.

You can provide custom initializers when you want to provide an easy way to let callers provide initialization values. This makes instance creation much easier (see Listing 41-3).

Listing 41-3. Custom Initializers

```
class Person {
    var name: String
    var age:Int

    func profile() -> String {
        return "I'm \(self.name) and I'm \(self.age) years old."
    }

    init() {
        self.name = "Name"
        self.age = 0
    }

    init(name:String, age:Int) {
        self.name = name
        self.age = age
    }

}

var p = Person(name: "Matt", age: 40)
```

In Listing 41-3, when you called the custom initializer, you had to provide the external name for each parameter. External names are descriptive prefixes designed to make code clear. Swift provides these for you automatically with init methods. Xcode will use these for code completion assistance.

Chapter 42

De-initialization

When an instance is no longer need, Swift deallocates the instance and frees up the instance resources. For the most part, this is an automatic process that you don't need to worry about when you are using standard Swift types. However, if you are using resources that need to be manually freed up (such as open files), you can de-initialize these resources by overriding the deinit method (see Listing 42-1).

Listing 42-1. deinit Method

```
class Person {
    var name: String = "Name"
    var age:Int = 0

    func profile() -> String {
        return "I'm \(self.name) and I'm \(self.age) years old."
    }

    deinit {
        //Remove any resources outside of standard
        //types and objects here
    }

}
```

In Listing 42-1, you added the deinit so you can include any additional resources that need to be deallocated.

> **Note** Creating resources that require deinit is beyond the scope of this book since Swift is very good at managing typical resources.

Chapter 43

Type Casting

You can convert value types such as floating-point and integer numbers to other types in Swift. This is called *type casting*. Obviously, if you convert a Double type to a Float or Int type, you will lose some precision in your numbers. Listing 43-1 shows some examples of how you might convert a floating-point number to other value types.

Listing 43-1. Type Casting Value Types

```
let f1 = 9.99
let i1 = Int(f1)
let d1 = Double(f1)
let b1 = Bool(f1)
let s1 = toString(f1)
```

In Listing 43-1, you type cast f1 to an integer, double, and boolean. In the last line, you converted f1 to a String type.

Type Casting Instances

You can type cast instances using the as keyword. Let's say you are using the Person and Employee classes from Chapter 39 and you've already created a new Employee instance, as shown in Listing 43-2.

Listing 43-2. Employee Instance

```
class Person {
    var name: String = "Name"
    var age:Int = 0

    func profile() -> String {
        return "I'm \(self.name) and I'm \(self.age) years old."
    }
}
```

```
    func doPersonThings() {
        println("\(self.name) is doing person things...")
    }

}

class Employee: Person {
    var employeeNumber = 1234567890
    var hourlyRate = 12.00

    func doEmployeeThings() {
        println("\(self.name) is doing employee things...")
    }
}

var e1 = Employee()
```

In Listing 43-2, you may notice that the two classes now include the new methods doPersonThings() and doEmployeeThings(). Also, you've created a new instance called e1 that can use both of the new methods (Listing 43-3).

Listing 43-3. Using Employee Methods

```
var e1 = Employee()
e1.name = "Jim"

e1.doPersonThings()
e1.doEmployeeThings()
```

In Listing 43-3, since Jim is an employee, his instance can use both doEmployeeThings() and doPersonThings().

The output from Listing 43-3 would look like this:

```
Jim is doing person things...
Jim is doing employee things...
```

There may be some situations where you want to use Jim's instance only as a Person. Maybe you have an array of instances you know for sure are People instances. While this array may have instances that are Employee instances, you can't be sure. So, you instead want to cast the objects in the array as People (see Listing 43-4).

Listing 43-4. Type Casting Instances

```
var e1 = Employee()
e1.name = "Jim"

e1.doPersonThings()
e1.doEmployeeThings()

let a1 = [e1]

for item in a1 {
    let p = item as Person
    p.doPersonThings()
}
```

If you attempted to add p.doEmployeeThings() in the loop in Listing 43-4, you would have gotten an error because you have access only to the methods available to the Person class now. This is called *down casting* when you type cast to a parent class (or any class higher in the class hierarchy).

Chapter **44**

Nested Types

When you are working with value types such as enumerations (Chapter 19), structures (Chapter 30), and reference types like classes (Chapter 31), you can nest other types in your type definitions. This means your class definition may include other class definitions, structure definitions, and enumeration definitions. Each of these may contain their own nested types.

For instance, if you wanted to expand the construct of a `Person` to include health information, you might do something like Listing 44-1.

Listing 44-1. Nested Classes

```
class Person {
    var name: String = "Name"
    var age:Int = 0
    var health = Health()

    func profile() -> String {
        return "I'm \(self.name) and I'm \(self.age) years old."
    }

    class Health {
        var pulse:Int = 100
        var bmi:Int = 20

        func profile() -> String {
            return "Pulse:\(self.pulse), BMI:\(self.bmi)"
        }
    }

}

let p = Person()

p.health.profile()
```

In Listing 44-1, you added a Health class definition right inside the class definition for Person. Since you added a health property inside the class definition, you also have a way to play with an example of a Health instance. The last line of code from Listing 44-1 produces this output:

```
Pulse:100, BMI:20
```

You could also add more organization to the structure you started in Chapter 30 (see Listing 44-2).

Listing 44-2. Nested Structures

```
struct Shapes {

    struct Rectangle {
        var x:Int = 0
        var y:Int = 0
        var width:Int = 0
        var height:Int = 0
    }

    struct Circle {
        let pi:Float = 3.1415
        var radius:Float = 0.0
    }
}

var c = Shapes.Circle()
c.radius = 45.0
```

In Listing 44-2, you have two types of shapes under the Shapes structure. You can reference nested types using dot syntax. You are free to mix, match, and nest types as you see fit as you create your programs.

Chapter 45

Extensions

You use *extensions* when you want to add methods and computed properties to a class, structure, or enumeration that already exists. This comes in handy when you want new behavior for a type but only in a particular context. Extensions will remind Objective-C programmers of categories.

To extend a type, you use the `extension` keyword followed by the name of the type you want to extend, as shown in Listing 45-1.

Listing 45-1. Extending the Person Class

```
class Person {
    var name: String = "Name"
    var age:Int = 0

    func profile() -> String {
        return "I'm \(self.name) and I'm \(self.age) years old."
    }

}

extension Person {
    var dogYears:Int {
    get{
        return self.age * 7
    }
    }
}

var p = Person()
p.name = "Matt"
p.age = 40

println(p.dogYears)
```

As you can see in Listing 45-1, you just need to use the extension keyword followed by the name of the class. Once you have that in place, you can add your computed properties, methods, initializers, subscripts, and other type definitions. In the last line of code, you printed the information from the new computed property dogYears, which is 280.

Chapter 46

Protocols

When you want to specify properties, methods, and types that would require other types to implement, you can use protocols. A protocol can be adopted by a type. *Adopting* a protocol means that a type will agree to implement the definition defined in the protocol.

To define a protocol, use the protocol keyword (see Listing 46-1).

Listing 46-1. Defining a Protocol

```
protocol PrinterProtocol {
    func printThis()
}
```

In Listing 46-1, you coded a new protocol named PrinterProtocol, which defined a function named printThis(). If you coded a class that you wanted to adopt this protocol, you would write the code shown in Listing 46-2.

Listing 46-2. Adopting a Protocol

```
class aClass:PrinterProtocol {

}
```

In Listing 46-2, you defined a class that adopted the PrinterProtocol protocol. When you adopt a protocol, the protocol name goes after the class name and a colon (:). If the class is also inheriting another class, you must list the protocol name after the parent class. For instance, if aClass inherited the Person class, you would need to use the code in Listing 46-3.

Listing 46-3. Protocol and Inheritance

```
class aClass: Person, PrinterProtocol{

    var i = 0

    func printThis() {
        println("Implement printThis for aClass")
    }
}
```

You may have noticed that your playground is displaying a build error. You should see a red disc in the left gutter. If you click the red disc, you'll see the message Type 'aClass' does not conform to protocol 'PrinterProtocol'. This error appears because you haven't yet implemented the function printThis(). Fix that now (see Listing 46-4).

Listing 46-4. Implementing Protocols

```
protocol PrinterProtocol {
    func printThis()
}

class aClass:PrinterProtocol {
    func printThis() {
        println("Implement printThis for aClass")
    }
}

var obj = aClass()

obj.printThis()
```

The error should have gone way for you if you followed the code from Listing 46-4. Protocols require only that you match the definition specified in the protocol. The actual implementation that you choose is entirely up to you.

The code from Listing 46-4 would result in this console log output:

```
Implement printThis for aClass
```

When you use protocols to specify variables, you must include the getter and/or setter definitions (Listing 46-5).

Listing 46-5. Protocol Properties

```
protocol PrinterProtocol {
    func printThis()
    var i:Int {get set}
}

class aClass:Person, PrinterProtocol {

    var i = 0

    func printThis() {
        println("Implement printThis for aClass & i = \(self.i)")
    }
}

var obj = aClass()

obj.printThis()
```

In Listing 46-5, you required a property i and then implemented i in the aClass class. The output from Listing 46-5 would look like this:

```
Implement printThis for aClass & i = 0
```

Chapter 47

Delegation

Delegation is a design pattern where one object asks another object for help. Protocols (Chapter 46) are an important part of delegation because protocols define how an object will be helped.

Delegation works by defining a protocol that will list all the methods and properties an object will need help with. Another object, known as the *delegate*, will provide the help needed by adopting and implementing the protocol. Objects ask for help by sending messages to their delegates.

To demonstrate delegation, imagine that you are working on a project management application and you've defined two classes: Project and Task. A Project instance manages a list of Task instances (see Listing 47-1).

Listing 47-1. Project Manager Classes

```
class Project {
    var name = ""
    var listOfTasks = [Task]()
}

class Task {
    var name = ""
    var done = false
}

var p = Project()
p.name = "Cook Dinner"

let taskNames = ["Choose Menu", "Buy Groceries", "Prepare Ingredients",
"Cook Food"]
```

```
for name in taskNames{
    var t = Task()
    t.name = name
    p.listOfTasks.append(t)
}
```

In Listing 47-1, you defined the Project and Task classes. Then you created a Project instance: p. Finally, you used an array of strings to create four tasks and add each task to p.

Implementing Delegation

Let's say you want to implement delegation for your project application that includes the Project object and Task instances. In your app, Task instances may need help from the Project instance. For instance, when a Task status is marked as Done, the task may not know what to do next. The task could ask the Project instance for help if Project was capable of acting as the Task's delegate.

Defining a Protocol

To act as a Task delegate, you need to first define a protocol for Task that defines the ways that Task will need help (see Listing 47-2).

Listing 47-2. Define TaskDelegate

```
protocol TaskDelegate{
    func taskStatusHasChanged(task:Task, done:Bool)
}

class Project {
    var name = ""
    var listOfTasks = [Task]()
}

class Task {
    var name = ""
    var done = false
}
```

In Listing 47-2, you defined a protocol named TaskDelegate that defined one function required to act as a delegate for a Task instance. In Listing 47-2, you had to include the TaskDelegate protocol definition before the class definitions because you will be using TaskDelegate in Project.

Adopting the Protocol

Since `Project` instances will be acting as delegates for `Task` instances, you will need to adopt the `TaskDelegate` protocol in your `Project` class (see Listing 47-3).

Listing 47-3. Adopting TaskDelegate

```
protocol TaskDelegate{
    func taskStatusHasChanged(task:Task, done:Bool)
}

class Project:TaskDelegate {
    var name = ""
    var listOfTasks = [Task]()
}

class Task {
    var name = ""
    var done = false
}
```

Implement Protocol

Now that you have adopted `TaskDelegate`, you must implement the methods defined in the protocol. Until you do that, you will see an error in the playground (see Listing 47-4).

Listing 47-4. Implementing TaskDelegate Methods

```
protocol TaskDelegate{
    func taskStatusHasChanged(task:Task, done:Bool)
}

class Project:TaskDelegate {
    var name = ""
    var listOfTasks = [Task]()
    func taskStatusHasChanged(task:Task, done:Bool){
        let status = (task.done ? "DONE" : "IN PROGRESS")
        println("Task \(task.name) is now \(status)")
    }
}

class Task {
    var name = ""
    var done = false
}
```

In Listing 47-4, you implemented the method from the `TaskDelegate` protocol. This method prints a notification to the console log when a `Task` status has changed. Now, you will need to set up `Task` to be able to use a delegate.

Adding Delegate Property

For `Task` instances to be able to ask for help, they will need to be able to reference a delegate property (see Listing 47-5).

Listing 47-5. Delegate Property

```
protocol TaskDelegate{
    func taskStatusHasChanged(task:Task, done:Bool)
}

class Project:TaskDelegate {
    var name = ""
    var listOfTasks = [Task]()
    func taskStatusHasChanged(task:Task, done:Bool){
        let status = (task.done ? "DONE" : "IN PROGRESS")
        println("Task \(task.name) is now \(status)")
    }
}

class Task {
    var name = ""
    var delegate:TaskDelegate?
        var done = false
}
```

In Listing 47-5, you added an optional property delegate. This is the instance that you will use as the delegate. You will want to use this delegate every time the Done status changes, so this is a good place to implement a custom getter and setter (see Listing 47-6).

Listing 47-6. Calling Delegate

```
protocol TaskDelegate{
    func taskStatusHasChanged(task:Task, done:Bool)
}

class Project:TaskDelegate {
    var name = ""
    var listOfTasks = [Task]()
    func taskStatusHasChanged(task:Task, done:Bool){
        let status = (task.done ? "DONE" : "IN PROGRESS")
        println("Task \(task.name) is now \(status)")
    }
}
```

```
class Task {
    var name = ""
    private var _done = false
    var delegate:TaskDelegate?
    var done:Bool {
        get {
            return _done
        }
        set {
            _done = newValue
            self.delegate?.taskStatusHasChanged(self, done: _done)
        }
    }
}
```

In Listing 47-6, you defined a custom getter and setter for the done property. In the setter for done, you made a call to the delegate letting the delegate know that the task status has changed. You also passed the delegate a reference to the task (using the self) keyword.

> **Note** The self keyword is used to reference an instance from a definition. So, when you use self in a class definition, the self keyword refers to the instance created from the class definition.

Assigning Delegate Property

For each task, you must assign the delegate property to the project instance. For this example, this is best done in the for loop where you created each task (see Listing 47-7).

Listing 47-7. Assigning Delegates

```
var p = Project()
p.name = "Cook Dinner"

let taskNames = ["Choose Menu", "Buy Groceries", "Prepare Ingredients",
"Cook Food"]

for name in taskNames{
    var t = Task()
    t.name = name
    t.delegate = p
    p.listOfTasks.append(t)
}
```

Using Delegation

To test your delegation pattern, change the task status of one of your tasks and examine the console log (see Listing 47-8).

Listing 47-8. Testing Delegation

```
p.listOfTasks[0].done = true
```

In Listing 47-8, you changed the status of the first task to complete.
The project instance was notified and printed this output to the console log:

```
Task Choose Menu is now DONE
```

> **Note**   This Delegation pattern as code will lead to a strong reference cycle (see Chapter 49), which means that a memory leak could occur because Task instances are maintaining references to the top-level Project instances. See Chapter 49 for more information about this, along with tips on how to resolve strong reference cycles.

Chapter 48

Generics

When you are working with types such as Int or String in Swift, you typically must declare the type or have the type inferred from the value. While this pattern makes some code clearer, sometimes you want to be able to use any type in your code. *Generics* gives you a way of doing just this.

To use generics, you must add <T> after a function name. Then you can substitute T in place of the type name. For example, let's say you are working with your Person and Employee classes from Chapter 40. Maybe you decide that you want to add a function to print information about the types of instance that you could have. Listing 48-1 shows how you can use generics to create one function for both types of instances.

Listing 48-1. Using Generics

```swift
class Person {
    var name: String = "Name"
    var age:Int = 0

    func profile() -> String {
        return "I'm \(self.name) and I'm \(self.age) years old."
    }
}

class Employee: Person {
    var employeeNumber = 1234567890
    var hourlyRate = 12.00

    override func profile() -> String {
        return "I'm \(self.name) and my hourly rate is $\(self.hourlyRate)"
    }
}
```

```
var p1 = Person()

p1.name = "Matt"
p1.age = 40

var e1 = Employee()

e1.name = "Jim"
e1.age = 18
e1.employeeNumber = 1
e1.hourlyRate = 15.55

func printPerson<T>(p:T){
    let o = p as Person
    println(o.profile())
}

printPerson (p1)
printPerson (e1)
```

In Listing 48-1, you added a function after setting up the Person and Employee classes and instances. Your function takes any instance and prints the instance profile. The output from Listing 48-1 would look like this:

```
I'm Matt and I'm 40 years old.
I'm Jim and my hourly rate is $15.55
```

Type Checking

The function from Listing 48-1 works great as long as you use the function only with Person or Employee instances. However, if you attempt to use this function with another type, you would get a runtime EXC_BAD_ACCESS error.

To avoid this type of error, you can add type checking to the function. Type checking is a way to test an instance to see whether it is a particular type. With type checking, you can say "Is this a Person instance?" Listing 48-2 shows how you would add type checking to your function.

Listing 48-2. Type Checking

```
func printPerson<T>(p:T){
    if p is Person || p is Employee{
        let o = p as Person
        println(o.profile())
    }
    else{
        println("\(p) is not a supported type.")
    }
}
```

```
printPerson (p1)
printPerson (e1)

var s = "ABC"
printPerson(s)
```

In Listing 48-2, you use the is keyword along with the OR logical operator
(| |) to test to see whether p is a Person or an Employee.

The function prints an employee or person profile or an error message if p is
neither of these types. Here is the output that Listing 48-2 would produce:

```
I'm Matt and I'm 40 years old.
I'm Jim and my hourly rate is $15.55
ABC is not a supported type.
```

Chapter **49**

Automatic Reference Counting

As your Swift program creates new instances, memory resources are used to store the information associated with each instance. When an instance is no longer needed, Swift will reclaim the resources associated with the instance so that these resources can be used with other instances.

The system that Swift uses to keep track of all your instances is called *automatic reference counting* (ARC). ARC works because Swift can keep a count of how many times an instance is referenced in a program. This is called the *reference count*. For the most part, you don't need to manage this yourself since Swift takes care of reference counting automatically.

> **Note** In Chapter 42, you coded a `deinit`, which is a special method that executes right before Swift disposes of an object. This method is called when an instance reference count is zero. When an instance reference count is zero, there are no remaining references to the instance.

Strong References and Reference Cycles

When a property is defined in a class, the class is said to have a strong relationship with the property. This means that instances of the class will increase the property's reference count in ARC. When the instance's reference count reaches zero and the instance is disposed of, any properties with strong references will be decreased by one.

ARC runs into a problem when you have classes reference each other. Take your `Project` and `Task` from Chapter 47 as an example. Listing 49-1 shows a simplified example of that relationship.

Listing 49-1. Project-Task Reference Cycle

```
import Foundation

class Project {
    var name = ""
    var listOfTasks = [Task]()
    deinit {
        println("\(self.name) project is being deinitialized")
    }
}

class Task {
    var name = ""
    private var _done = false
    var parent:Project?
    deinit {
        println("\(self.name) task is being deinitialized")
    }
}

var p:Project? = Project()
p!.name = "Cook Dinner"

let taskNames = ["Choose Menu", "Buy Groceries", "Prepare Ingredients",
"Cook Food"]

for name in taskNames{
    var t = Task()
    t.name = name
    t.parent = p
    p!.listOfTasks.append(t)
}

p = nil
```

> **Note** To follow along with this example, you will need to create a command-line tool Mac application (see Chapter 3). You need the command-line application because playgrounds always maintain a reference to instances regardless of what you do, so you will never see the deinitialization messages unless you are using an application.

In Listing 49-1, you have coded two classes, Project and Task, each of which have deinit methods that will execute right before these instances are disposed of.

> **Note**   Instead of a delegate property in Task, you have a property named parent, which is an optional Project type that a Task instance may use to get information about the project that the Task instance belongs to. Finally, when you instantiate your Project and Task instances, you declare the Project instance as optional. You declare Project as optional because you need to set this instance to nil at the end to dispose of the instance.

When you build and run the application in Listing 49-1, it seems to run fine. But, if you look at the console log, you will notice that no messages were written out even though you expected some. This means the code in deinit was never reached and these five Task instances were never disposed of. This is a memory leak.

You could solve this problem by removing the line of code that assigns the Project instance to the parent property for each Task instance (Listing 49-2).

Listing 49-2. Removing Strong Reference

```
var p:Project? = Project()
p!.name = "Cook Dinner"

let taskNames = ["Choose Menu", "Buy Groceries", "Prepare Ingredients",
"Cook Food"]

for name in taskNames{
    var t = Task()
    t.name = name
    //t.parent = p
    p!.listOfTasks.append(t)
}

p = nil
```

When you comment out the line from Listing 49-2, you will get the following output in the console log:

```
Cook Dinner project is being deinitialized
Choose Menu task is being deinitialized
Buy Groceries task is being deinitialized
Prepare Ingredients task is being deinitialized
Cook Food task is being deinitialized
```

This demonstrates the problem, but this is not a great solution because each Task instance may need to reference the parent Project at times. Swift helps you with the weak keyword for properties. By adding the weak keyword, you are telling the class to not maintain a strong relationship to the property. This means the parent instance will not increase the property's reference count (see Listing 49-3).

Listing 49-3. Weak References

```
import Foundation

class Project {
    var name = ""
    var listOfTasks = [Task]()
    deinit {
        println("\(self.name) project is being deinitialized")
    }
}

class Task {
    var name = ""
    private var _done = false
    weak var parent:Project?
    deinit {
        println("\(self.name) task is being deinitialized")
    }
}

var p:Project? = Project()
p!.name = "Cook Dinner"

let taskNames = ["Choose Menu", "Buy Groceries", "Prepare Ingredients",
"Cook Food"]

for name in taskNames{
    var t = Task()
    t.name = name
    t.parent = p
    p!.listOfTasks.append(t)
}

p = nil
```

In Listing 49-3, you added the weak keyword to the parent Project property. You were also able to assign the Project instance to each Task instance without creating a strong reference cycle or creating a memory leak.

The output shown here would still look correct and verify that no memory leak is occurring, and you would still get the needed reference:

```
Cook Dinner project is being deinitialized
Choose Menu task is being deinitialized
Buy Groceries task is being deinitialized
Prepare Ingredients task is being deinitialized
Cook Food task is being deinitialized
```

Index

Get the eBook for only $10!

Now you can take the weightless companion with you anywhere, anytime. Your purchase of this book entitles you to 3 electronic versions for only $10.

This Apress title will prove so indispensible that you'll want to carry it with you everywhere, which is why we are offering the eBook in 3 formats for only $10 if you have already purchased the print book.

Convenient and fully searchable, the PDF version enables you to easily find and copy code—or perform examples by quickly toggling between instructions and   applications. The MOBI format is ideal for your Kindle, while the ePUB can be utilized on a variety of mobile devices.

Go to www.apress.com/promo/tendollars to purchase your companion eBook.

Apress®
THE EXPERT'S VOICE™

CPSIA information can be obtained at www.ICGtesting.com
Printed in the USA
LVOW07s0840151214

418884LV00001B/203/P